Standardized Test Practice Handbook
with Answer Key

The American Nation

HOLT, RINEHART AND WINSTON

A Harcourt Classroom Education Company

Austin · New York · Orlando · Atlanta · San Francisco · Boston · Dallas · Toronto · London

The American Nation

Standardized Test Practice Handbook
with Answer Key

Acknowledgments

Project Editor: Carol Alexander
Executive Editor: Karen Bischoff
Senior Editor: Carol Traynor
Editors: Amy Robbins
 Debra Tursi
Design Director: Steve Coleman
Design Associate: Jean-Paul Vest
Production: Jan Jarvis/Willow Graphics

Grateful acknowledgment is made to the following for permission to use copyrighted material:

Page 6, **Test-Taking Strategies** by Marren Simmons and Marlene Roth from *Keys to Excellence*. Copyright © by Steck-Vaughn/Berrent Publications. Reprinted by permission of the authors.

Copyright © by Steck-Vaughn Company

All rights reserved. No part of this publication may be reproduced or transmitted in any form or by any means, electronic or mechanical, including photocopy, recording, or any information storage and retrieval system, without permission in writing from the publisher.

Teachers using *The American Nation* may photocopy complete pages in sufficient quantities for classroom use only and not for resale.

Printed in the United States of America

ISBN 0-03-064277-9

1 2 3 4 5 6 7 8 9   145   02 01 00 99

Table of Contents

About the Program...5
Test-Taking Strategies..6
Specific Objectives...9

Part 1: Activities

Activity 1	Reading Comprehension: Prehistory	10
Activity 2	Reading Vocabulary: Empires of the Americas	12
Activity 3	Language: Life in Colonial Massachusetts	14
Activity 4	Social Science: Independence!	16
Activity 5	Reading Comprehension: From Confederation to Federal Union	18
Activity 6	Reading Vocabulary: A Strong Start for the Nation	20
Activity 7	Language: Nathaniel Hawthorne	22
Activity 8	Social Science: Regional Societies	24
Activity 9	Reading Comprehension: Women and Reform	26
Activity 10	Reading Vocabulary: Expansion and Conflict	28
Activity 11	Language: The Abolitionist Movement	30
Activity 12	Social Science: The Civil War	32
Activity 13	Reading Comprehension: Reconstruction and the New South	34
Activity 14	Reading Vocabulary: The Western Crossroads	36
Activity 15	Language: The Second Industrial Revolution	38
Activity 16	Social Science: The Transformation of American Society	40
Activity 17	Reading Comprehension: The Populist Movement	42
Activity 18	Reading Vocabulary: The Age of Reform	44
Activity 19	Language: Progressive Politicians	46
Activity 20	Social Science: America and the World	48
Activity 21	Reading Comprehension: The United States Goes to War	50
Activity 22	Reading Vocabulary: A Turbulent Decade	52
Activity 23	Language: Henry Ford	54
Activity 24	Social Science: Prosperity Shattered	56
Activity 25	Reading Comprehension: Life in the New Deal Era	58
Activity 26	Reading Vocabulary: The Road to War	60
Activity 27	Language: World War II	62
Activity 28	Social Science: The Cold War	64
Activity 29	Reading Comprehension: The Challenges of Peace	66
Activity 30	Reading Vocabulary: The New Frontier and the Great Society	68
Activity 31	Language: Martin Luther King Jr. and the Civil Rights Movement	70
Activity 32	Social Science: Struggles for Change	72
Activity 33	Reading Comprehension: War in Vietnam	74
Activity 34	Reading Vocabulary: From Nixon to Carter	76
Activity 35	Language: Women in the Military	78
Activity 36	Social Science: Life in the 1990s and Beyond	80
Activity 37	Reading Comprehension: Industrialism and Empire	82

Activity 38	Reading Vocabulary: The Rise of the Global Economy	84
Activity 39	Language: The Movement of People and Ideas	86
Activity 40	Social Science: The Struggle for Human Rights	88

Part 2: Practice Tests
Practice Test 1:	Reading Comprehension	90
Practice Test 2:	Reading Vocabulary	98
Practice Test 3:	Language	100
Practice Test 4:	Social Science	106
Practice Test 5:	Listening	112

Part 3: Answer Key
Listening Passages and Questions	114
Answers	118
Student Answer Sheet	131

About the Program

The American Nation Standardized Test Practice Handbook has been developed to refresh basic skills, familiarize students with test formats and directions, and teach test-taking strategies for standardized tests. Developed in conjunction with Holt, Rinehart and Winston's in-depth American history program, *The American Nation*, the *Handbook* provides social studies teachers with a way for their students to hone their skills at taking standardized tests, while at the same time drawing on the material that students are studying in class.

Format of the Book

The *Standardized Test Practice Handbook* is divided into three sections:

Part 1: Activities

This section includes 40 Activities, covering the full sweep of American history. The Activities rotate among and assess the four content areas of Reading Comprehension, Reading Vocabulary, Language, and Social Science. The questions included for each Activity cover the skills evaluated on standardized tests.

Included in the first four Activities in this section are:
- **Sample**—an example given to familiarize students with test-taking items
- **Try This**—a skill strategy for students that enables them to approach the Activity in a logical manner
- **Think It Through**—a specific explanation of the correct answer for the Sample item

Part 2: Practice Tests

This section includes five Practice Tests—Reading Comprehension, Reading Vocabulary, Language, Social Science, and Listening—that are based on the material in *The American Nation* and modeled on the kinds of test items found on standardized tests. The Practice Tests in the *Standardized Test Practice Handbook* give students an opportunity to take a test under conditions that parallel those they will face when taking standardized tests.

Part 3: Answer Key

This section includes the Listening passages and questions for Practice Test 5: Listening, as well as an Answer Key for all the multiple-choice and open-ended questions.

How to Answer Questions

The *Handbook* consists of multiple-choice and open-ended questions. In Part 1, the Activity lessons, multiple-choice answers should be filled in at the bottom of each page and open-ended questions should be written in the space provided. For the Practice Tests in Part 2, students should answer multiple-choice questions on the two-page Answer Sheet found on pages 131 and 132. Open-ended questions should continue to be answered in the space provided on each page.

Test-Taking Strategies

The following strategies demonstrate ways to help you organize information when taking standardized reading tests. These three strategies enable you to analyze what you need to know in order to successfully answer specific kinds of reading questions.

Strategy 1: Check and See

This strategy is used when a question asks you to identify a fact or detail found in the selection. The correct answer is stated directly in the text. You do not need to generalize or infer the answer. Sometimes the actual words from the text are used in the answer choices.

Check and See will enable you to answer questions that require you to remember specific details or information. It is used when you are asked to locate facts from the selection.

The *Check and See* Strategy

1. **Read:** Read the question and determine what you are actually being asked.

2. **Find:** Find the information given in the selection.

3. **Decide:** Decide which strategy you need to use.

Check and See: Put a check next to the sentence that contains the information needed in order to answer the question.

4. **Answer:** Select the choice that best answers the question.

Strategy 2: Puzzle Piece

This strategy is used when a question asks you to determine what something means. Often the actual answer is implied in the selection. It is not stated directly in the text. You have to read the material and infer information or draw a conclusion in order to select the correct answer.

Puzzle Piece will help you infer information and piece the facts together. This method is similar to putting together a puzzle. You must have all the pieces in front of you in order to do the puzzle. You need to find the missing facts before you can complete the picture and answer the questions.

The *Puzzle Piece* Strategy

1. **Read:** Read the question and determine what you are actually being asked.

2. **Find:** Find the information given in the selection.

3. **Decide:** Decide which strategy you need to use.

Write: Write down the facts as if they are pieces in a puzzle.
Solve: Solve the puzzle by piecing together what you have inferred.

4. **Answer:** Select the choice that best answers the question.

Strategy 3: What Lights Up?

This strategy is used when additional information is needed in order to answer a question. You need to go further than what is stated or implied in the selection. You need to add your own personal experiences or thoughts to what you are reading.

What Lights Up helps you evaluate what you are reading. You can determine what information is useful or necessary in order to select an answer. It allows you to include personal insights, make predictions, and extend the meaning of the text itself. Often these kinds of questions are the most difficult to answer. This strategy will help you create meaningful responses that go beyond what is written in the selection.

The *What Lights Up* Strategy

1. Read: Read the question and determine what you are actually being asked.

2. Find: Find the information given in the selection.

3. Decide: Decide which strategy you need to use.

Think: Think about your own personal thoughts and experiences.
Light Up: Your own ideas will light up the answer in your mind.

4. Answer: Select the choice that best answers the question.

Specific Objectives

Reading Comprehension

Objective 1: Determining word meanings
Words with multiple meanings, prefixes and suffixes, context clues, and technical words

Objective 2: Identifying supporting ideas
Sequential order and following directions

Objective 3: Summarizing main ideas
Stated and implied main ideas and identifying summaries

Objective 4: Perceiving relationships and recognizing outcomes
Cause-and-effect and making predictions

Objective 5: Making inferences and generalizations
Interpreting graphs and diagrams, inferring information, drawing conclusions, making judgments, and evaluating cause/effect relationships

Objective 6: Recognizing points of view, facts, and opinions
Author's purpose and persuasive language

Reading Vocabulary

Objective 1: Determining word meaning

Objective 2: Matching words with more than one meaning

Objective 3: Using context clues

Language

Objective 1: Prewriting, composing, and editing

Objective 2: Identifying misspelled words

Listening

Objective 1: Understanding word meaning

Objective 2: Building listening skills

NAME _____ CLASS _____ DATE _____

Part 1: Activities

Activity 1 Reading Comprehension: Prehistory

Directions: Darken the circle for the correct answer, or write your answer in the space provided.

TRY THIS — Read each selection and each question twice. Check your answers by looking back in the selection.

Sample A

As the mammoths and other large game died out, the Paleo-Indians were forced to develop new skills in order to survive. Paleo-Indians experimented with new types of hunting and trapping. The men and women of the Eastern Woodlands, for example, learned to burn large areas of forest to make it easier to spot and track smaller game such as rabbit and deer.

As large game such as mammoths died out, the Paleo-Indians—

A gradually died out in most areas of North America.

B adopted a vegetarian diet.

C developed new types of hunting and trapping.

D migrated to new territories.

THINK IT THROUGH — The correct answer is <u>C</u>. The third choice explains that the Paleo-Indians adapted to the changing environment by finding new ways of obtaining food.

The Changing Environment

Sometime between 10,000 and 5,000 B.C., the climate of the Americas grew warmer and drier. This climatic change dramatically transformed the landscape. Continents were left much as they would later appear to the first European explorers. Scientists believe that as the climate changed, some Paleo-Indians moved south. In a migration that took thousands of years, they spread throughout the Americas and established distinct cultures in various regions.

Because none of the Native American tribes of that era kept written records, much of their history is lost to us. One way we can learn about early Native Americans, however, is through the work of archaeologists. These scientists study ancient artifacts and ruins in order to learn about the people who made them. Other scientists piece together early American history by studying modern-day Native Americans, including the myths and legends that had been handed down by previous generations. After all, most Native American cultures preserved their histories through the telling of stories. Scholars gain important clues to understanding the Paleo-Indians with their study of these oral records.

Most Native American myths reveal something about their past. For example, a popular myth offers an explanation of what happened to the Paleo-Indians after some time on the American continent.

"For a long time everyone spoke the same language, but suddenly people began to speak in different tongues. Kulsu [the Creator], however, could speak all languages, so he called the people together and told them the names of the animals in their own language, taught them to get food, and gave them their laws and rituals. Then he sent each tribe to a different place to live."

From a Maidu creation myth from "The Big-Game Vanishes," *Kingdoms of Gold, Kingdoms of Jade: The Americas Before Columbus*, by Brian M. Fagan. Published by Thames & Hudson, 1991.

NAME _____ CLASS _____ DATE _____

1. **The migration of Paleo-Indians occurred mainly as a result of—**
   A the development of new agricultural methods.
   B climate changes throughout the Americas.
   C the increasing sophistication of stone weaponry.
   D the extinction of mammoths and other large game.

2. **In this selection, the word <u>artifacts</u> means—**
   F prehistoric sculptures.
   G oral histories of prehistoric tribes.
   H cultural variations.
   J objects crafted by humans.

3. **The Native American myth quoted in the passage explains—**
   A why different languages and cultures developed.
   B why the Paleo-Indians worshipped the god Kulsu.
   C how environment shaped human evolution.
   D the organization of hunter-gatherer societies.

4. **What else do we learn about this Native American culture from the myth quoted in the passage?**
   F Tribal people were not concerned with recording their history.
   G The identification of animals was very important to Native American peoples.
   H Native American peoples all worshipped the same god.
   J Native American tribes were unable to communicate with one another.

5. **Why do we have so little information about prehistoric Native American peoples?**
   A There are no artifacts left from this era.
   B Native Americans did not pass on many myths to their descendants.
   C Native Americans did not keep written records.
   D Archaeologists lack the technology to study such ancient cultures.

6. **What kinds of information do scientists gather from early myths and legends?**
   _____
   _____
   _____
   _____
   _____

7. **What changes in the environment of the Americas occurred between 10,000 and 5,000 B.C.?**
   F The climate remained stable.
   G The climate grew warmer and drier.
   H Huge glaciers covered the continent.
   J Mammoths and other large game populations increased.

8. **Why did distinct differences exist between various Paleo-Indian tribes?**
   _____
   _____
   _____
   _____
   _____

1 Ⓐ Ⓑ Ⓒ Ⓓ   3 Ⓐ Ⓑ Ⓒ Ⓓ   5 Ⓐ Ⓑ Ⓒ Ⓓ   7 Ⓕ Ⓖ Ⓗ Ⓙ
2 Ⓕ Ⓖ Ⓗ Ⓙ   4 Ⓕ Ⓖ Ⓗ Ⓙ   6 Open-ended   8 Open-ended

11

Activity 2 Reading Vocabulary: Empires of the Americas

Directions: Darken the circle for the correct answer, or write your answer in the space provided.

| TRY THIS | Read the sentence in the box. Decide what the underlined word means. Then find the word or words with nearly the same meaning. |

Sample A

> Native people could not <u>arrest</u> the spread of unknown diseases.

Which word or group of words means the same, or almost the same, as the underlined word in the sample sentence?

A diagnose accurately

B describe

C live comfortably with

D stop

| THINK IT THROUGH | The correct answer is <u>D</u>. Choice <u>D</u> has nearly the same meaning as the word <u>arrest</u>. |

1 The word <u>viceroy</u> means—

  A royalty.

  B supervisor.

  C governor.

  D admiral.

2 > The larger Caribbean islands had more <u>complex</u> social and political organizations.

  In which sentence does <u>complex</u> have the same meaning as it does in the sentence above?

  F A <u>complex</u> sentence has an independent and at least one dependent clause.

  G Our town has a brand new movie theater <u>complex</u>.

  H He exhibited all of the signs of an inferiority <u>complex</u>.

  J Further study is needed of our <u>complex</u> ecosystems.

3 Christopher Columbus believed the good-hearted Taino could be easily <u>subjugated</u> and forced to submit and obey. <u>Subjugated</u> means—

  A conquered.

  B imitated.

  C corrupted.

  D confounded.

4 The word <u>heritage</u> means—

  F refuge.

  G history.

  H traditions.

  J liberty.

5 European diseases proved particularly deadly because American Indians had no <u>immunity</u> to them. <u>Immunity</u> means—

A resistance.
B knowledge.
C medicines.
D hostility.

6 What does the word <u>malnutrition</u> mean?
_____
_____
_____

7 Many American Indians <u>succumbed</u> to unfamiliar diseases such as smallpox and measles. <u>Succumbed</u> means—

F avoided.
G died.
H spread.
J received.

8
> "Of all my country," Mexican poet Sor (Sister) Juana Inés de la Cruz wrote, "I was the <u>venerated</u> figure, one of the idols that inspire the general applause."
>
> From "Los Empeños de una Casa" by Sor Juana Inés de la Cruz, translated by Fanchón Royer, from "The Cell That Became an Academy" from *The Tenth Muse: Sor Juana Inés de la Cruz*, by Fanchón Royer. Published by St. Anthony Guild Press, Patterson, NJ 1952.

<u>Venerated</u> means—

A despised.
B subdued.
C honored.
D neglected.

9 The word <u>esteem</u> means the same as—

F consider.
G estimate.
H engage.
J congratulate.

10 What does the word <u>emaciated</u> mean?
_____
_____
_____

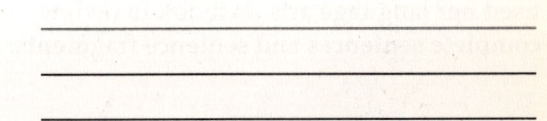

5 Ⓐ Ⓑ Ⓒ Ⓓ   7 Ⓕ Ⓖ Ⓗ Ⓙ   9 Ⓕ Ⓖ Ⓗ Ⓙ
6 Open-ended 8 Ⓐ Ⓑ Ⓒ Ⓓ   10 Open-ended

NAME _____ CLASS _____ DATE _____

Activity 3 Language: Life in Colonial Massachusetts

Directions: Darken the circle for the correct answer, or write your answer in the space provided.

TRY THIS — Imagine that you are Rebecca, the student mentioned below. Use the rules you have learned for capitalization, punctuation, word usage, and sentence structure to choose the correct answer.

Sample A

Rebecca enjoyed reading about the founding of the colony of Massachusetts Bay. She plans to write a summary of what she has learned. Rebecca realizes it is necessary to begin organizing information from the material she has read.

What should Rebecca do before she starts to write her summary?

A Look up the spellings of any unfamiliar words in the material.

B Find out how Massachusetts has changed over the past three centuries.

C Study an atlas for information about Massachusetts today.

D Make some notes about important points in her reading.

THINK IT THROUGH — The correct answer is D. The first thing Rebecca should do is make notes about key ideas and details in her reading. It is important to look for main points and supporting details in order to write a clear summary.

While Rebecca was writing her summary, she used her language arts textbook to review complete sentences and sentence fragments.

1 Which group of words is not a whole sentence?

   A The colonists believed all people were responsible to the community.

   B Native Americans helped the people of the young colony.

   C Hoped to find fertile land and a temperate climate.

   D Children also had many responsibilities in the new colony.

14   SA Ⓐ Ⓑ Ⓒ Ⓓ   1 Ⓐ Ⓑ Ⓒ Ⓓ

Directions: Rebecca is writing a summary of what she has learned about life in the Massachusetts Bay colony. Here is a rough draft of Rebecca's summary. Read the rough draft carefully. Darken the circle for the correct answer, or write your answer in the space provided.

The colony of Massachusetts was founded by the Puritans in 1630. These immigrants (1) (2) had a special purpose. Their leader, John Winthrop, expressed the idea that the colony (3) would be a model for the world. "We must consider that we shall be as a city upon (4) a hill. The eyes of all people are upon us." This sense of mission was displayed by many (5) (6) of the laws and customs that characterized the Massachusetts Bay Colony laws such as those governing literacy, education, and social behavior were stringent in comparison with those of other colonies. Life in the southern colonies was much different. (7)

Cooperation between church and state were essential in the Puritan community. (8) In all ways. This emphasis on morality and responsibility to the community was (9) (10) known as the New England Way. The village meeting-house was a center for both (11) religious and public activities.

---

2 What would be the best topic sentence for paragraph 1?

F In each colony throughout North America, a unique set of laws and customs prevailed.

G The people of Massachusetts had great faith in the power of religion.

H John Winthrop was a strong and popular leader.

J The Puritans brought their high moral and ethical principles to the colony they founded in Massachusetts.

3 Which sentence in paragraph 1 is a run-on sentence?

A 1
B 3
C 6
D 7

4 What is the best way to rewrite sentence 8?

_____
_____
_____
_____

---

2 Ⓕ Ⓖ Ⓗ Ⓙ   3 Ⓐ Ⓑ Ⓒ Ⓓ   4 Open-ended   15

NAME _____ CLASS _____ DATE _____

Activity 4 Social Science: Independence!

Directions: Darken the circle for the correct answer, or write your answer in the space provided.

TRY THIS — Read the sentence in the box. Decide which answer best summarizes the sentence.

Sample A

> Why did tensions build rapidly between the American colonists and the British?

A The colonists sought more aid from King George and Parliament.

B The British Crown demanded too much revenue from the colonists.

C Too many British subjects wished to emigrate to the colonies.

D Americans misunderstood British feeling toward the colonies.

THINK IT THROUGH — The correct answer is B. Choice B be summarizes the source of trouble between the colonists and Great Britain. There is no information in the lesson to support the other answers.

---

1. Pontiac's Rebellion was an example of—

   A anti-British feeling among the colonists.

   B a major battle of the French and Indian War.

   C American Indian uprisings.

   D a rebellion of slaves against plantation owners.

2. The effect of the Stamp Act of 1765 was to—

   F impose an import tax on sugar and molasses.

   G tax printed matter circulating in the American colonies.

   H limit the business of rum distillers and ship owners.

   J arrest colonists who attempted to smuggle goods into the country.

3. The colonists staged the Boston Tea Party because—

   A they feared the East India Company would monopolize the tea trade.

   B they wanted to start an open war of independence against Great Britain.

   C the British would no longer supply the American colonies with tea.

   D the tax on tea was higher than the tax on other luxury imports.

4. What problems did the Continental Army encounter during the winter of 1777–78?

   _____
   _____
   _____
   _____

---

16   SA ⓐ ⓑ ⓒ ⓓ   1 ⓐ ⓑ ⓒ ⓓ   3 ⓐ ⓑ ⓒ ⓓ
                  2 ⓕ ⓖ ⓗ ⓙ   4 Open-ended

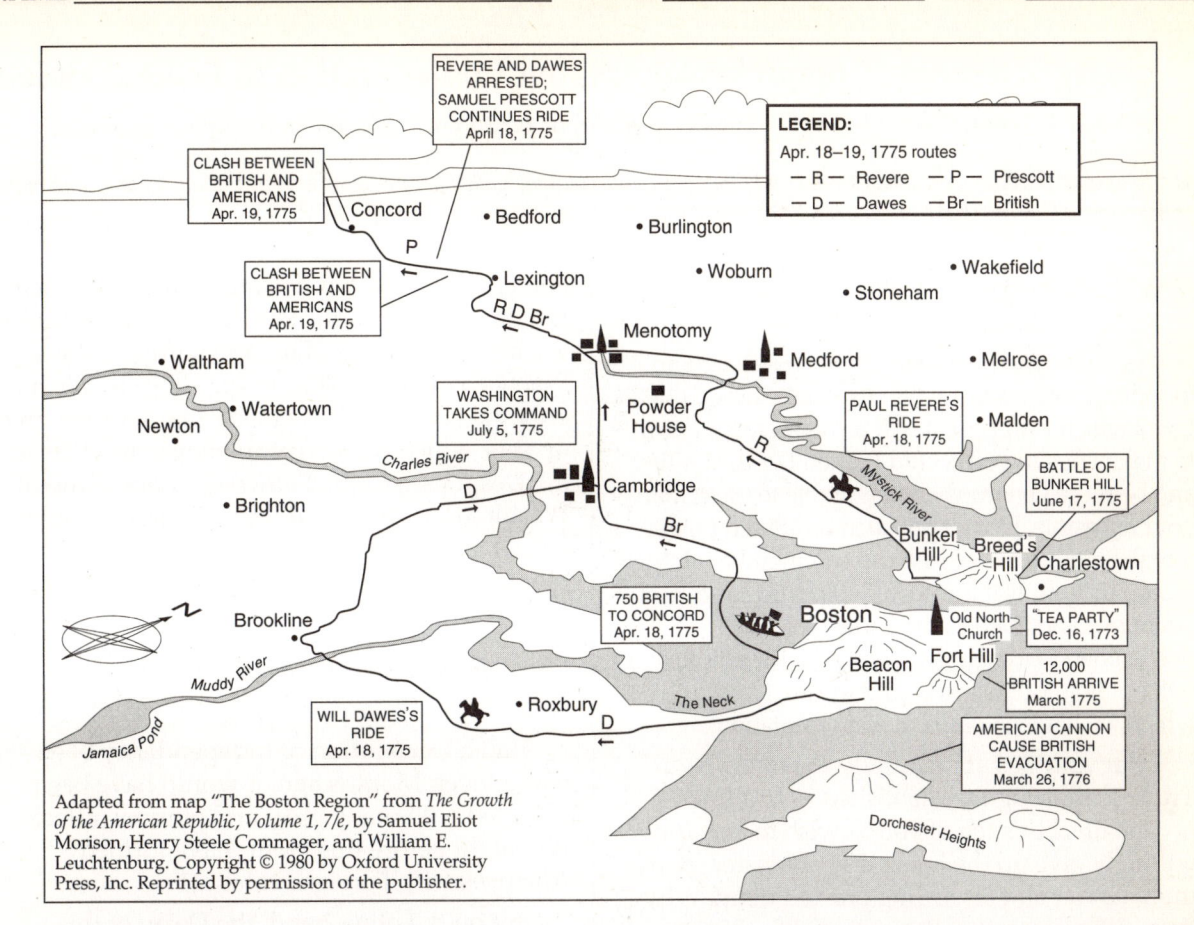

5 According to the map above, which bodies of water did Will Dawes have to cross on his ride?

  F the Muddy River and the Charles River
  G Boston Harbor and the Mystick River
  H the Muddy River and Boston Harbor
  J the Mystick River and the Charles River

6 Why did the colonists protest the British Crown's decision to pay the salaries of the governor and judges of Massachusetts directly?

  A The British Crown wanted to lower the salaries of these officials.
  B The British pound was worth less than American currency.
  C The colonists feared these officials would be free to ignore colonial demands.
  D The colonists wanted complete independence from Britain.

> "When the people are oppressed, when their Rights are infringed, when their property is invaded, when taskmasters are set over them ... in such circumstances the people will be discontented, and they are not to be blamed."

7 The above quotation from Samuel Adams refers to—

  F the decimation of American Indian populations in the West.
  G early protests of slavery by northern abolitionists.
  H religious discrimination against the Scotch-Irish in Britain.
  J Britain's attempts to impose certain taxes on the colonists.

Activity 5 Reading Comprehension: From Confederation to Federal Union

Directions: Darken the circle for the correct answer, or write your answer in the space provided.

The following selections are taken from letters written while colonial leader John Adams was in Philadelphia as a member of the Second Continental Congress and his wife, Abigail Adams, was managing the family farm in Massachusetts.

Abigail Adams to John Adams
Braintree, March 31, 1776

. . . —I long to hear that you have declared an independency—and by the way in the new Code of Laws which I suppose it will be necessary for you to make I desire you would Remember the Ladies, and be more generous and favorable to them than your ancestors. Do not put such unlimited power into the hands of the Husbands. Remember all Men would be tyrants if they could. If particular care and attention is not paid to the Ladies we are determined to foment [encourage] a Rebellion, and will not hold ourselves bound by any Laws in which we have no voice, or Representation.

That your Sex are naturally Tyrannical is a Truth so thoroughly established as to admit of no dispute, but such of you as wish to be happy willingly give up the harsh title of Master for the more tender and endearing one of Friend. Why then, not put it out of the power of the vicious and the Lawless to use with cruelty and indignity with impunity. Men of Sense in all Ages abhor those customs which treat us only as the vassals [servants] of your Sex. Regard us then as Beings placed by providence under your protection and in imitation of the Supreme Being make use of that power only for our happiness.

John Adams to Abigail Adams, April 14, 1776

As to your extraordinary Code of Laws, I cannot but laugh. We have been told that our Struggle has loosened the bonds of Government everywhere. That Children and Apprentices were disobedient—that schools and Colleges were grown turbulent—that Indians slighted their Guardians and Negros grew insolent to their Masters. But your Letter was the first Intimation [hint] that another Tribe more numerous and powerful than all the rest were grown discontented. —This is rather too coarse a Compliment but you are so saucy, I won't blot it out.

Depend upon it, We know better than to repeal our Masculine systems. Although they are in full Force, you know they are little more than Theory. We dare not exert our Power in its full Latitude. We are obliged to go fair, and softly, and in Practice you know We are the subjects. We have only the Name of Masters, and rather than give up this, which would completely subject Us to the Despotism of the Petticoat, I hope General Washington, and all our brave Heroes would fight. I am sure every good Politician would plot, as long as he would against Despotism, Empire, Monarchy, Aristocracy . . .

John Adams to Abigail Adams
Philadelphia, July 3, 1776

Had a Declaration of Independency been made seven Months ago, it would have been attended with many great and glorious Effects . . . We might before this Hour, have formed Alliances with Foreign States . . .

But on the other hand, the Delay of this Declaration to this Time, has many great Advantages attending it.—The Hopes of Reconciliation, which were fondly entertained by Multitudes of honest and well meaning though weak and mistaken People, have been gradually and at last totally extinguished . . . The Second Day of July 1776, will be the most memorable Epoch [date] in the History of America—I am apt to believe that it will be celebrated, by succeeding Generations, as the great anniversary Festival. It ought to be commemorated, as the Day of Deliverance by solemn Acts to Devotion to God Almighty. It ought to be solemnized [honored] with Pomp [ceremony] and Parade, with Shews [exhibits], Games, Sports, Guns, Bells, Bonfires, and Illuminations from one End of this Continent to the other from this Time forward forevermore.

You will think me transported [carried away] with Enthusiasm but I am not.—I am well aware of the Toil and Blood and Treasure [money], that it will cost Us to maintain this Declaration, and support and defend these States.

From *The Book of Abigail and John: Selected Letters of the Adams Family, 1762-1784.* L. H. Butterfield et al., eds. Harvard University Press, 1975.

NAME _____ CLASS _____ DATE _____

1. **The purpose of Abigail Adams's letter to her husband is—**
   A to complain about his unfair treatment of herself and their children.
   B to persuade him to support laws giving legal rights to women.
   C to inform him that the women of the country are in a state of rebellion.
   D to argue that women are the more just and logical sex.

2. **When Abigail Adams writes, "Men of Sense in all Ages abhor those customs which treat us only as the vassals of your Sex," she means—**
   F reasonable men do not dominate or mistreat women.
   G husbands of all ages are guilty of being tyrants.
   H throughout history, men have treated women as servants.
   J men have been responsible for developing customs that dishonor women.

3. **In paragraph 2 of Abigail Adams's letter, what does the word <u>impunity</u> mean?**
   A impudence
   B having legal authority
   C without fear of punishment
   D without thought or deliberation

4. **Why do you think Abigail Adams put her thoughts about the equality of women into a letter to her husband?**
   _____
   _____
   _____

5. **In John Adams's letter of April 14, the "Struggle" he refers to is—**
   F the battle of the sexes.
   G the first battle of the American Revolution.
   H the economic problems of the colonies.
   J the colonists' efforts to achieve independence from Britain.

6. **What does John Adams refer to when he says, "But your Letter was the first Intimation that another Tribe more numerous and powerful than all the rest were grown discontented"?**
   A the uprisings of American Indians throughout the colonies
   B the increasing anger of the colonists toward the British Crown
   C the growing desire of women for legal and social equality
   D the difficulty of restraining the Patriots from opening fire on British soldiers

7. **What is the main point of Adams's letter of April 14?**
   F Men know that they do not actually dominate or control women.
   G Most men prefer their theories about women to reality.
   H Men are more concerned with political struggles than with domestic troubles.
   J Men will never surrender their control over their wives.

8. **In Adams's letter of July 3, we learn that—**
   A he fears the colonists will lose the war.
   B he thinks the Declaration of Independence was made too late.
   C he thinks victory is only a few months away.
   D he believes loyalists to be politically weak and misguided.

1 Ⓐ Ⓑ Ⓒ Ⓓ   3 Ⓐ Ⓑ Ⓒ Ⓓ   5 Ⓕ Ⓖ Ⓗ Ⓙ   7 Ⓕ Ⓖ Ⓗ Ⓙ
2 Ⓕ Ⓖ Ⓗ Ⓙ   4 Open-ended   6 Ⓐ Ⓑ Ⓒ Ⓓ   8 Ⓐ Ⓑ Ⓒ Ⓓ

Activity 6 Reading Vocabulary: A Strong Start for the Nation

Directions: Darken the circle for the correct answer, or write your answer in the space provided.

1. The word <u>reluctant</u> means the same as—
   A eager.
   B unwilling.
   C divided.
   D contrary.

2. What does the word <u>ratification</u> mean?
   _____
   _____
   _____
   _____

3. | The people's representatives needed to make <u>critical</u> decisions about policies and procedure. |

   In which sentence does <u>critical</u> have the same meaning as it does in the sentence above?
   F The general was <u>critical</u> of some of the enlisted men.
   G The members of the Second Continental Congress gave the document a <u>critical</u> reading.
   H The author was upset over a <u>critical</u> review of her latest book.
   J George Washington's leadership was considered <u>critical</u> to the success of the Patriots.

4. The word <u>validity</u> means—
   A soundness.
   B probability.
   C quality.
   D organization.

5. The editor Philip Freneau stated, "A system of finance has been issued from the Treasury of the United States and has given rise to scenes of speculation calculated to <u>aggrandize</u> the few and the wealthy, by oppressing the great body of the people." <u>Aggrandize</u> means—
   F antagonize.
   G increase.
   H reduce.
   J influence.

6. In 1796 President Washington decided that he would not seek a third term, thus setting a <u>precedent</u> for later presidents. The word <u>precedent</u> means—
   A a limitation imposed by law.
   B a difficult situation.
   C a pledge or promise.
   D an act that is used as an example.

7. The word <u>incongruous</u> means the same as—
   F inappropriate.
   G unethical.
   H unsuccessful.
   J ridiculous.

1 Ⓐ Ⓑ Ⓒ Ⓓ   3 Ⓕ Ⓖ Ⓗ Ⓙ   5 Ⓕ Ⓖ Ⓗ Ⓙ   7 Ⓕ Ⓖ Ⓗ Ⓙ
2 Open-ended   4 Ⓐ Ⓑ Ⓒ Ⓓ   6 Ⓐ Ⓑ Ⓒ Ⓓ

8   The word <u>ultimately</u> means—

A   softly or stealthily.

B   eventually or finally.

C   often or usually.

D   early or originally.

9
> The novelist Catharine Maria Sedgwick described how over time, "the wigwams which constituted the village . . . gave place to the clumsy, but more convenient dwellings of the pilgrims."

In which sentence does <u>constituted</u> have the same meaning as it does in the sentence above?

F   The new government <u>constituted</u> many laws protecting individual rights.

G   John Marshall was <u>constituted</u> Chief Justice of the United States.

H   A speech and a luncheon <u>constituted</u> the proceedings of our club.

J   The American presidency was <u>constituted</u> in 1789.

10 What does the word <u>impressment</u> mean?

_____
_____
_____
_____

11 The Shoshoni guide and interpreter, Sacagawea, proved <u>invaluable</u> to the Lewis and Clark expedition. <u>Invaluable</u> means the same as—

A   impractical.

B   worthless.

C   important.

D   trivial.

Activity 7 Language: Nathaniel Hawthorne

Directions: Gerald is writing an analysis of passages from Nathaniel Hawthorne's "Sights from a Steeple." Here is a part of a rough draft of Gerald's analysis. Read the rough draft carefully. Darken the circle for the correct answer, or write your answer in the space provided.

As we read this sketch of a New England town. We gain insight into both the
(1) (2)
narrator and the town that is the object of his study. The narrator's position is
(3)
ideally suited to offer an overview of this village in the 1800s. His knowledge
(4)
of the community makes him a good commentator.

The narrator's survey of his town and its inhabitants had revealed a busy
(5)
community intent on work and social pleasures. This is a port town commercial
(6)
shipping is its main business. The narrator points out "vessels unloading at the
(7)
wharf, and precious merchandise strewn upon the ground . . ." He observes what
(8)
seems to be a group of merchants at the door of a warehouse. This is apparently
(9)
the business center of the town.

Hawthorne if he is the narrator takes a keen interest in personal relations.
(10)
He prefers to observe, though, commenting that "The most desirable mode of
(11)
existence might be that of a spiritual Paul Pry, hovering invisible round man
and woman . . ." Likewise, the narrator finds the social scene interesting. His gaze
(12) (13)
follows two young women and a man. Are they flirting with one another?
(14)
Do they know each other well? The narrator does not know, just looks on with
(15) (16)
great curiosity.

22

NAME _____ CLASS _____ DATE _____

1. **Which group of words in paragraph 1 is not a whole sentence?**
   A 1
   B 2
   C 3
   D 4

2. **Which sentence in paragraph 1 needlessly repeats an idea from a previous sentence?**
   F 1
   G 2
   H 3
   J 4

3. **What is the topic sentence of paragraph 2?**
   A 5
   B 6
   C 7
   D 9

4. **Which sentence in paragraph 2 is a run-on sentence?**
   F 5
   G 6
   H 7
   J 8

5. **In sentence 5, what is the best way to rewrite had revealed?**
   A has revealed
   B reveal
   C reveals
   D As it is written.

6. **In sentence 10, what is the best way to punctuate Hawthorne if he is the narrator?**
   F Hawthorne, if he is the narrator,
   G Hawthorne, if he is the narrator:
   H Hawthorne, if he is the narrator?
   J As it is written.

7. **What is the best way to rewrite sentence 17?**
   _____
   _____
   _____
   _____
   _____

8. **Which sentence is an appropriate conclusion to paragraph 3?**
   A Many fascinating things go on in a small town.
   B The narrator must not have many acquaintances in the community.
   C The people he observes appear to be wealthy.
   D His detached viewpoint marks the narrator as a natural writer.

9. **What would be a good title for Gerald's essay?**
   _____
   _____
   _____
   _____

1 Ⓐ Ⓑ Ⓒ Ⓓ   3 Ⓐ Ⓑ Ⓒ Ⓓ   5 Ⓐ Ⓑ Ⓒ Ⓓ   7 Open-ended   9 Open-ended
2 Ⓕ Ⓖ Ⓗ Ⓙ   4 Ⓕ Ⓖ Ⓗ Ⓙ   6 Ⓕ Ⓖ Ⓗ Ⓙ   8 Ⓐ Ⓑ Ⓒ Ⓓ

Activity 8 Social Science: Regional Societies

Directions: Darken the circle for the correct answer, or write your answer in the space provided.

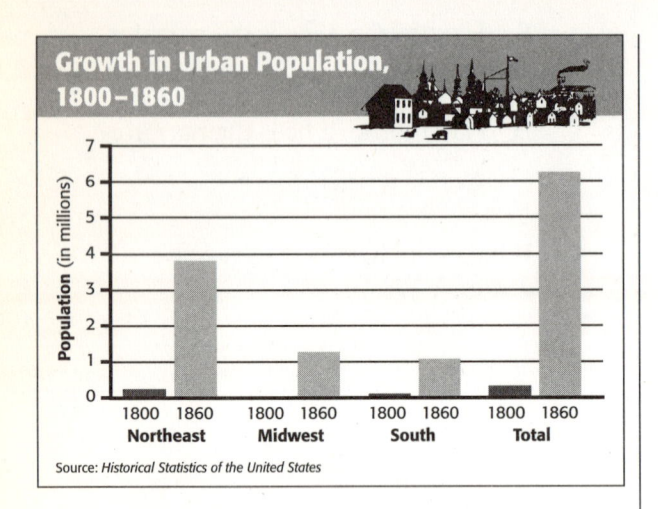

Growth in Urban Population, 1800–1860

Source: *Historical Statistics of the United States*

1. According to the graph, which of the following developments took place between 1800 and 1860?

   A Northeastern urban populations remained constant during this period.

   B The growth in urban populations in the Midwest and South was identical.

   C The urban population in the Midwest declined between 1800 and 1860.

   D The South had the slowest growth in urban population.

2. The Market Revolution came about as a result of—

   F the rise of the middle class.

   G the factory system.

   H the increase in the number of small shops.

   J the sudden growth of cities in the southern states.

3. The main reform brought about by labor unions in the 1830s was—

   A the reduction of the workday to ten hours.

   B a sharp rise in wages for factory workers.

   C an end to child labor in factories.

   D an increase in the number of jobs in the textiles industry.

4. In the 1800s, the largest group of immigrants to the United States were—

   F German Jews.

   G German Protestants.

   H Irish Catholics.

   J English Catholics and Protestants.

5. The "Know-Nothings" were—

   A immigrants who did not yet speak the English language.

   B a nativist group with strong anti-Catholic feelings.

   C Irish Catholics who formed close-knit communities.

   D New York City politicians.

6. Which of these developments was responsible for the continuation of slavery and the plantation system?

   F Eli Whitney's invention of the cotton gin

   G the Market Revolution

   H the enormous influx of immigrants into the country

   J the fall of tobacco prices in the early 1800s

NAME _____ CLASS _____ DATE _____

7 **How did the majority of white southerners make their living?**

    A by managing large plantations

    B by working in manufacturing

    C by small-scale farming

    D by engaging in professions such as medicine and law

8 **Before the outbreak of the Civil War, slavery was—**

    F practiced only on large plantations in the South.

    G practiced in urban centers as well as rural areas.

    H practiced only in regions where cotton was grown.

    J illegal in the Upper South.

9 **The system known as "gang labor" involved—**

    A the use of convicts as slaves.

    B the practice of using children to work in the cotton fields.

    C the use of over fifty slaves on an individual plantation.

    D the assignment of slaves into specialized jobs.

10 **In what important ways did northern and southern economies differ?**

_____
_____
_____
_____
_____
_____

7 Ⓐ Ⓑ Ⓒ Ⓓ   9 Ⓐ Ⓑ Ⓒ Ⓓ
8 Ⓕ Ⓖ Ⓗ Ⓙ   10 Open-ended

Activity 9 Reading Comprehension: Women and Reform

Directions: Darken the circle for the correct answer, or write your answer in the space provided.

Reform in the 1800s

Most women who joined reform efforts during the early 1800s were members of the new middle class that had emerged as a result of economic changes in the United States. The wives and daughters of this new class of merchants and professionals were at the forefront of efforts to improve social and moral conditions in the young nation. Middle- and upper-class women often hired domestic servants to maintain their households. This allowed them the leisure time to become involved in reform issues.

Many women of this period believed that, as females, they had a particular duty to become involved in social reform. The so-called cult of true womanhood that developed from the emphasis on women's responsibilities within the home actually led some middle-class women to expand their roles beyond the household. Women's growing sense of moral and civic responsibility led them to establish associations dedicated to improving society and uplifting its citizens. Women also argued that if they were to serve as the moral leaders of their families, then they must be allowed to acquire the educational skills and training to do so.

The expansion of women's education was part of a widespread effort to improve education in America. Prior to the 1840s most schools were private, and most families could not afford to send their children. The few public elementary schools that existed—most of them in the Northeast—had little money for books, supplies, or teachers' salaries. The curriculum was basic: reading, writing, arithmetic, and some history and geography. Furthermore, the quality of teaching in public schools was generally poor. Attendance was irregular. Many students received only a few years of schooling.

Reformers worried that the existing schools were inadequate to meet the needs of the growing nation. They argued that the nation needed public, tax-supported elementary schools to provide a free education to all children. Reformers insisted that schools were essential to educate citizens about democratic values, to heal social divisions, and to create a literate and disciplined workforce. The schools could achieve these goals, reformers hoped, by teaching a basic curriculum and instilling in students the middle-class values of hard work and respect for authority.

Horace Mann's reform efforts in Massachusetts established a model for free public elementary education. In 1837, as Massachusetts's first secretary of education, Mann united local school districts into a state system, raised teachers' salaries, and persuaded the legislature to increase spending on local schools. He also lengthened the school year, updated the curriculum, and established teacher training schools. Mann's school reforms soon spread throughout the United States. He convinced other educators that "the common [public] school, improved and energized, may become the most effective . . . of all the forces of civilization."

The public high school was another product of education reform during this period. The nation's first, the English High School of Boston, opened in 1821. Free public high schools offered children who could not afford private schools a chance to pursue advanced courses that could prepare them for specialized careers.

Educational reform had little impact on the South, however. Many northern educational reformers also supported the abolition of slavery, making many southerners suspicious of northern education reforms. As a result, the South was slow to adopt northern reforms. Planters hired private tutors or established private schools for their own children. They did not support the establishment of public schools to educate all children.

NAME _____ CLASS _____ DATE _____

1 The term "cult of true womanhood" refers to—
   A the developing interest of women in reform movements in the 1800s.
   B the increase in the number of educated American women.
   C the expectation that women would focus all their activities on household matters.
   D the involvement of women in religion and spiritualism.

2 Many reform associations in the 1800s were established by—
   F educational leaders such as Horace Mann.
   G upper-class southern women.
   H teachers in the nation's new public schools.
   J middle-class women.

3 In this selection, the word literate means—
   A able to read and write.
   B having a background in English literature.
   C cultured and genteel.
   D enrolled in elementary school.

4 Public school education in most of the nation expanded in the—
   F late 1800s.
   G mid 1800s.
   H 1840s.
   J early 1800s.

5 Northern reformers in the field of education advocated—
   A the creation of all-female high schools.
   B the establishment of tax-supported elementary schools.
   C the improvement of the nation's existing private schools.
   D the tutorial system for the nation's children.

6 When Horace Mann declared that the public schools "may become the most effective . . . of all the forces of civilization," what did he mean?
   F Public schools could provide a better education than private schools.
   G No civilization of the past had ever established public schools.
   H Public schooling would teach children to be civilized and polite.
   J An educated populace would be democratic and productive.

7 What might Horace Mann have hoped to accomplish by uniting local school districts in Massachusetts into a state system?
   _____
   _____
   _____
   _____

8 Before teacher training schools were established, the quality of education provided by American schools was probably—
   A adequate.
   B inadequate.
   C inferior.
   D superior.

1 Ⓐ Ⓑ Ⓒ Ⓓ   3 Ⓐ Ⓑ Ⓒ Ⓓ   5 Ⓐ Ⓑ Ⓒ Ⓓ   7 Open-ended
2 Ⓕ Ⓖ Ⓗ Ⓙ   4 Ⓕ Ⓖ Ⓗ Ⓙ   6 Ⓕ Ⓖ Ⓗ Ⓙ   8 Ⓐ Ⓑ Ⓒ Ⓓ

NAME _____   CLASS _____   DATE _____

Activity 10 Reading Vocabulary: Expansion and Conflict

Directions: Darken the circle for the correct answer, or write your answer in the space provided

1. Magazine editor John L. O'Sullivan wrote, "The American claim is by the right of our <u>manifest</u> destiny to overspread and to possess the whole of the continent which Providence has given us for the development of the great experiment of liberty." In this sentence, the word <u>manifest</u> means—

    A   national.

    B   obvious.

    C   united.

    D   multiple.

2. The word <u>tactic</u> means the same as—

    F   maneuver.

    G   texture.

    H   agreement.

    J   policy.

3.
> During the Texas Revolution, rebel William Travis called upon Americans "to come to our aid with all <u>dispatch</u>."

    In which sentence does <u>dispatch</u> have the same meaning as it does in the sentence above?

    A   The commander's <u>dispatch</u> reached the lieutenant too late to be of use.

    B   Each morning, the editor would <u>dispatch</u> the reporters to various sites.

    C   The business of the firing squad was to <u>dispatch</u> the condemned man.

    D   The messenger delivered the letter with <u>dispatch</u>.

4. Stories about the bravery of William Travis and his followers added to the <u>status</u> of the Alamo defenders, who would become legendary. In this sentence, <u>status</u> means—

    F   peril.

    G   prestige.

    H   mythical quality.

    J   tragedy.

5. The word <u>ensuing</u> means the same as—

    A   following.

    B   assured.

    C   illegal.

    D   preceding.

6. What does the word <u>renunciation</u> mean?

    _____
    _____
    _____
    _____

NAME _____ CLASS _____ DATE _____

7
> Spanish officials <u>promoted</u> immigration to California by recruiting artisan families to teach the American Indians of the missions blacksmithing, carpentry, and herding.

In which sentence does <u>promoted</u> have the same meaning as it does in the sentence above?

F The entire family celebrated on the day my mother was <u>promoted</u> to head supervisor.

G Missionaries <u>promoted</u> the conversion of some tribes to Christianity.

H Under the new policy, a student cannot be <u>promoted</u> without passing standardized tests in reading and mathematics.

J Reformers worked together to <u>promote</u> the general welfare of society.

8 The word <u>chastise</u> means—

A question.

B criticize.

C punish.

D chase.

9 What does the word <u>pandemonium</u> mean?

_____
_____
_____
_____

10 The word <u>destitute</u> means the same as—

F ignorant.

G embarrassed.

H diseased.

J penniless.

7 F G H J   9 Open-ended
8 A B C D   10 F G H J

29

Activity 11 Language: The Abolitionist Movement

Directions: Carlos is writing a report on the abolitionist movement. Here is a rough draft of the first part of Carlos's report. Read the rough draft carefully. Darken the circle for the correct answer, or write your answer in the space provided.

> In the years leading up to the Civil War, uneasy years in which tensions erupted.
> (1)
> The American people struggled with a huge problem. Should slavery continue in the
> (2) (3)
> nation? Should free people turn their eyes away from the cruel and unjust system
> (4)
> practiced throughout the South? One group of people the abolitionists said "No!"
> (5)
>
> Abolitionists had existed before the Fugitive Slave Act of 1850 it became a crime
> (6)
> to help runaway slaves, even outside the slave states. There were some abolitionists
> (7)
> in the South, too. This Act was included in the Compromise of 1850, a futile attempt
> (8)
> to prevent a showdown between the North and the South. Northern Abolitionists
> (9)
> reacted to this new law with horror.
>
> The abolition movement was ignited. Well-known orators such as ex-slave
> (10) (11)
> Frederick Douglass spoke against slavery and urging people to defy the new law.
>
> Some responded to this call forming mobs and freeing captured fugitives, helping
> (12)
> them to escape to Canada. Writers like Harriet Beecher Stowe wrote novels that
> (13)
> showed the evils of slavery. The Underground Railroad, a loose system of safe houses
> (14)
> and conductors who led slaves to freedom formed by individuals. Former slaves such
> (15)
> as Harriet Tubman became famous as skilled conductors who knew when and where
>
> to travel to reach the North.

30

NAME _____ CLASS _____ DATE _____

1. Which group of words in paragraph 1 is not a whole sentence?

   A 1
   B 2
   C 3
   D 4

2. In sentence 5, <u>the abolitionists said "No!"</u> should be written—

   F the abolitionists said; "No!"
   G , the abolitionists, said, "No!"
   H the abolitionists, said "No!"
   J As it is written.

3. What is the best way to rewrite sentence 6?

   _____
   _____
   _____

4. Which sentence in paragraph 2 is out of place?

   A 6
   B 7
   C 8
   D 9

5. Which sentence would best follow sentence 8?

   F Slavery in North America dated back to the early 1600s.
   G Pennsylvania was a border state between slavery and freedom.
   H It meant that slavery was expanding into the free territories.
   J Harriet Tubman was perhaps the best-known conductor on the Underground Railroad.

6. What is the best way to rewrite sentence 11?

   _____
   _____
   _____
   _____

7. In sentence 12, <u>responded to this call forming mobs</u> is best written—

   A responded to this call by forming mobs
   B responding to this call by forming mobs
   C responded to this call formed mobs
   D As it is written.

8. Which sentence in paragraph 3 should be moved to a later paragraph?

   F 10
   G 11
   H 12
   J 13

9. What is the best way to rewrite sentence 14?

   _____
   _____
   _____
   _____

1 Ⓐ Ⓑ Ⓒ Ⓓ   3 Open-ended   5 Ⓕ Ⓖ Ⓗ Ⓙ   7 Ⓐ Ⓑ Ⓒ Ⓓ   9 Open-ended
2 Ⓕ Ⓖ Ⓗ Ⓙ   4 Ⓐ Ⓑ Ⓒ Ⓓ   6 Open-ended   8 Ⓕ Ⓖ Ⓗ Ⓙ

NAME _____ CLASS _____ DATE _____

Activity 12 Social Science: The Civil War

Directions: Darken the circle for the correct answer, or write your answer in the space provided.

1. President-elect Abraham Lincoln responded to the Crittenden Compromise by—
   A declaring war on the southern secessionists.
   B speaking out against slavery as unconstitutional.
   C opposing the further expansion of slavery.
   D prohibiting slavery throughout the nation.

2. President Lincoln first called for federal troops to mobilize after—
   F the Confederates bombarded Fort Sumter.
   G seven states seceded from the union.
   H the Confederacy took over many federal forts, mints, and arsenals.
   J the Confederates named Richmond, Virginia, as their capital.

3. Delaware, Kentucky, Missouri, and Maryland were—
   A the first southern states to secede from the union.
   B slave states that did not secede from the union.
   C states with the highest concentration of slaves.
   D southern states in which slavery had long been banned.

4. Which of these facts best explains why the Confederacy had far fewer soldiers than the Union?
   F More than one-third of southerners were slaves.
   G The South was largely agrarian, while the North was industrialized.
   H In several southern states, pro-Union regiments were raised.
   J The mountain people of northwestern Virginia held few slaves.

5. Which famous military commander opposed secession yet fought on the southern side?
   A Ulysses S. Grant
   B Stonewall Jackson
   C Robert E. Lee
   D Jefferson Davis

6. The "Anaconda Plan" was the nickname of—
   F the federal government's naval blockade of the South.
   G Lincoln's strategy to reunite North and South.
   H the southern plan to capture Washington and invade the North.
   J West Virginia's resistance to the Confederacy.

7. By 1862, southern troops were undermined mainly because of—
   A lack of interest in the Confederate cause.
   B the obvious superiority of Union soldiers.
   C lack of food and supplies.
   D cunning spies working for the federal government.

NAME _____ CLASS _____ DATE _____

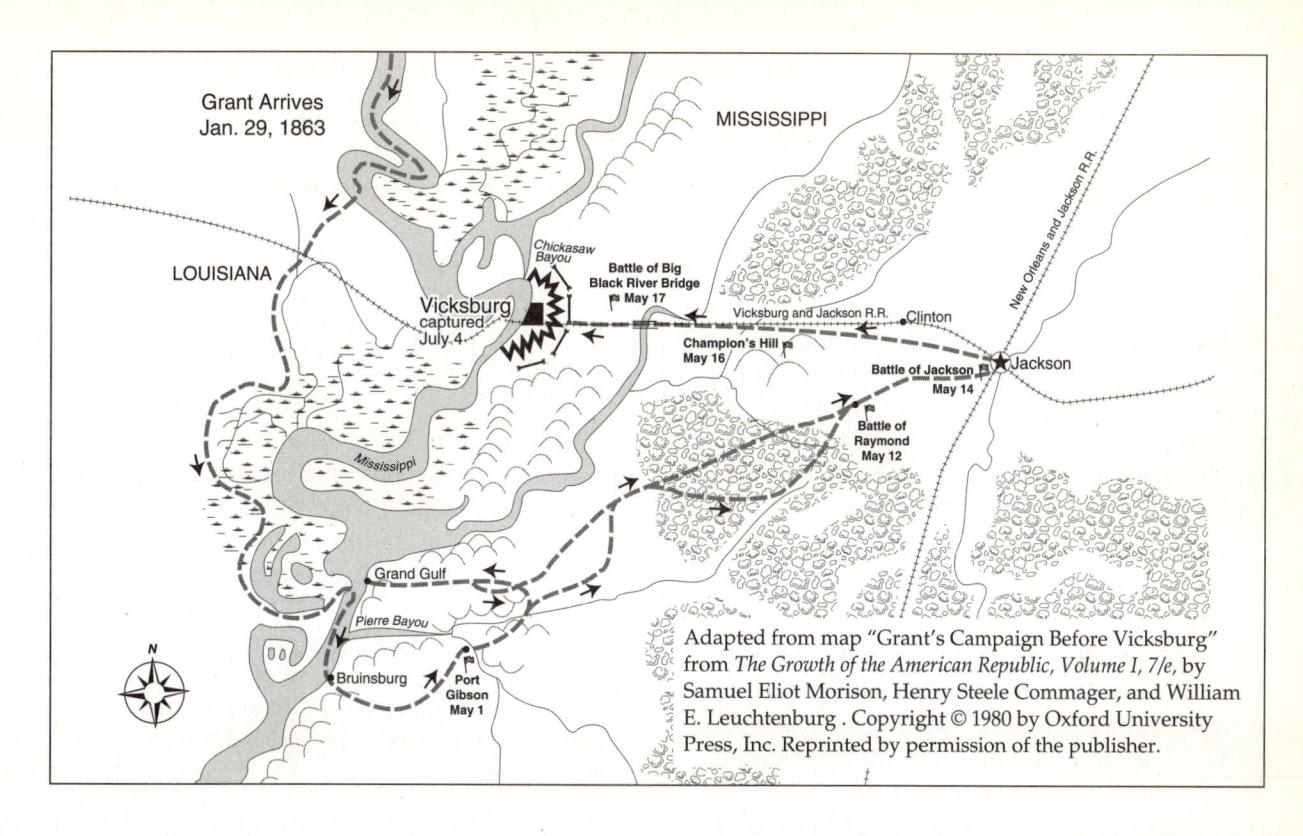

Map: Grant's Campaign Before Vicksburg

Grant Arrives Jan. 29, 1863
MISSISSIPPI
LOUISIANA
Chickasaw Bayou
Vicksburg captured July 4
Battle of Big Black River Bridge May 17
Vicksburg and Jackson R.R.
Clinton
New Orleans and Jackson R.R.
Champion's Hill May 16
Battle of Jackson May 14
Jackson
Battle of Raymond May 12
Mississippi
Grand Gulf
Pierre Bayou
Bruinsville
Port Gibson May 1

Adapted from map "Grant's Campaign Before Vicksburg" from *The Growth of the American Republic, Volume I, 7/e,* by Samuel Eliot Morison, Henry Steele Commager, and William E. Leuchtenburg. Copyright © 1980 by Oxford University Press, Inc. Reprinted by permission of the publisher.

8 According to the map, why was General Grant so determined to capture Vicksburg?

F The city of Vicksburg contained the largest number of Confederate troops.

G Vicksburg was the city closest to the Confederate capital at Richmond.

H Vicksburg lay in a mountainous area which effectively hid rebel fighters.

J The Union needed to gain control of the Mississippi River.

9 Why did General Lee invade Pennsylvania in 1863?

A He wanted to seize provisions from the enemy.

B He knew two Union brigades waited near Gettysburg, Pennsylvania.

C He hoped to reach a compromise with General Grant.

D Many Confederate victories had given him confidence.

10 Why did President Lincoln appoint Ulysses S. Grant as commander of all Union forces.

_____
_____
_____
_____
_____
_____
_____

8 F G H J   10 Open-ended
9 A B C D

33

Activity 13 Reading Comprehension: Reconstruction and the New South

Directions: Darken the circle for the correct answer, or write your answer in the space provided.

President Andrew Johnson and Reconstruction

After President Lincoln's death, Vice President Andrew Johnson assumed the presidency. Johnson was a Democrat, a one-time slaveholder, and a former U.S. senator from Tennessee. He had been chosen as Lincoln's running mate in 1864 because of his pro-Union sympathies. Republican leaders had hoped he would appeal to northern Democrats and southern Unionists.

Despite his support for the Union and his wartime experience as Tennessee's military governor, Johnson proved ill-suited to the challenges of Reconstruction and of defining African Americans' new rights. He favored a government controlled by white citizens. He also suffered, as one contemporary observer noted, from "almost unconquerable prejudices against the African race." Johnson also lacked Lincoln's political skill, often refusing to compromise.

In May 1865 Johnson issued a complete pardon to all rebels except former Confederate officeholders and the richest planters, whom he pardoned on an individual basis. Johnson's leniency extended to the rebel states as well. For readmission to the Union, his plan required only that they nullify their acts of secession, abolish slavery, and refuse to pay Confederate government debts. The last provision was intended to punish southerners who had financed the Confederacy.

Southerners, including General Robert E. Lee, enthusiastically supported President Johnson's plan, for it allowed Confederate leaders to take charge of Reconstruction. These men—some of whom continued to wear their army uniforms—dominated the new state legislatures. Even former Confederate vice president Alexander H. Stevens, who had been charged with treason, took office in the nation's capital as a representative.

These former Confederate lawmakers made sure that the new state constitutions did not grant voting rights to freed people. When the lawmakers complained of the "painful humiliation" inflicted by the presence of African American soldiers in the South, President Johnson had the troops removed. By recognizing Mississippi's new government, Johnson even overlooked the state's refusal to ratify the Thirteenth Amendment —which Congress had passed in January 1865 to abolish slavery.

President Johnson's actions encouraged former Confederates to adopt laws limiting the freedom of former slaves. These Black Codes closely resembled pre-Civil War codes. Mississippi, for example, simply recycled its old code, substituting the word "freedman" for "slave."

The Black Codes varied from state to state, but they all aimed to prevent African Americans from achieving social, political, and economic equality with southern whites. African Americans could not hold meetings unless whites were present. The code also forbade them to travel without permits, own guns, attend schools with whites, or sit on juries.

---

1 According to the passage, Andrew Johnson's background prepared him to be—

A hostile to the former Confederates.

B sympathetic to the former Confederates.

C impartial to both northern and southern concerns.

D ideally suited to the problems of the Reconstruction era.

2 In this passage, the word <u>contemporary</u> means—

F belonging to the same period of time.

G the present time period.

H a modern person.

J a person of about the same age.

34   1 Ⓐ Ⓑ Ⓒ Ⓓ
      2 Ⓕ Ⓖ Ⓗ Ⓙ

NAME _____ CLASS _____ DATE _____

3. **Why did Johnson require rebel states to refuse to pay Confederate government debts?**

   A to take worthless Confederate money out of circulation

   B to ensure that the economy of the South would be ruined

   C to impose financial penalties on supporters of the Confederacy

   D to help rebel states repair their economies as quickly as possible

4. **In the eyes of one observer, Johnson was particularly ill-equipped to handle issues relating to the freedmen because—**

   F he was extremely prejudiced against African Americans.

   G he was ignorant of the racial problems occurring in the South.

   H he believed whites and blacks would soon live in harmony.

   J he had no clear plan for Reconstruction of the South.

5. **In what way did Mississippi defy the federal law?**

   A The state actively promoted segregation.

   B The state did not cancel its acts of secession.

   C The state allowed former officers to wear their uniforms in public.

   D The state did not ratify the Thirteenth Amendment.

6. **How did most southerners regard President Johnson's approach to Reconstruction?**

   F with suspicion and fear

   G with cautious optimism

   H with great enthusiasm

   J with open hostility

7. **Why did Johnson remove African American troops from the South?**

   A He feared that the African American troops would fire on white civilians.

   B He was sympathetic to the feelings of prejudiced white citizens.

   C He foresaw that freedmen and whites would harm each other.

   D He wanted to protect the troops from the Black Codes.

8. **How did Johnson show that his Reconstruction policies were inconsistent and confused?**

   F He did not support the 1865 law abolishing slavery.

   G He showed an inability to compromise.

   H He insisted that rebel states ratify the Thirteenth Amendment.

   J He allowed high ranking ex-Confederates to hold political office.

9. **What was the aim of the Black Codes established by white southerners?**

   A to encourage former slaves to leave the South

   B to limit the freedom of African Americans

   C to create "separate but equal" opportunities for black and white southerners

   D to ensure that African Americans were treated fairly

10. **How might President Johnson's policies have angered northern Congressmen?**

    _____
    _____
    _____
    _____
    _____

3 Ⓐ Ⓑ Ⓒ Ⓓ   5 Ⓐ Ⓑ Ⓒ Ⓓ   7 Ⓐ Ⓑ Ⓒ Ⓓ   9 Ⓐ Ⓑ Ⓒ Ⓓ
4 Ⓕ Ⓖ Ⓗ Ⓙ   6 Ⓕ Ⓖ Ⓗ Ⓙ   8 Ⓕ Ⓖ Ⓗ Ⓙ   10 Open-ended

NAME _____ CLASS _____ DATE _____

Activity 14 Reading Vocabulary: The Western Crossroads

Directions: Darken the circle for the correct answer, or write your answer in the space provided.

1. The word <u>barbarity</u> means—
   A aggressive behavior.
   B hesitation.
   C cruel conduct.
   D resistance.

2. In 1874 the government <u>violated</u> the terms of the 1868 Treaty of Fort Laramie by sending an army expedition into the Black Hills to look for gold. <u>Violated</u> means—
   F observed.
   G altered.
   H transferred.
   J broke.

3. According to a social scientist of the late 1800s, the American Indian Ghost Dance religion was the expression of a <u>devastated</u> society. <u>Devastated</u> means—
   A overwhelmed.
   B ancient.
   C extinct.
   D primitive.

4. | Many experts believed that American Indians could survive only through <u>assimilation</u> into "white America." |

   In which sentence does <u>assimilation</u> have the same meaning as it does in the sentence above?
   F The <u>assimilation</u> of protein helps build muscle tissue.
   G The <u>assimilation</u> of Yan's parents was incomplete; they spoke their original language and did not mingle with their American neighbors.
   H Linguists study ways in which speech sounds are modified through <u>assimilation</u>.
   J Some tribes eat the organs of a slain foe because they believe they will become stronger through the <u>assimilation</u> of the enemy's vital force.

5. As the Great Plains were opened to farming, some companies created <u>bonanza</u> farms. The word <u>bonanza</u> refers to—
   A a ranch owned by the government.
   B privately-owned land.
   C a large-scale operation.
   D a farm run by immigrants.

36

NAME _____ CLASS _____ DATE _____

6 In October 1889 a flood of <u>prospective</u> settlers came to Oklahoma to claim free homesteads. <u>Prospective</u> means—

F likely to become.

G extremely capable.

H hardworking.

J cautiously approaching.

7
> When the government ordered the Nez Percé to relocate to a <u>reservation</u> in Idaho, their leader, Chief Joseph, reluctantly agreed.

In which sentence does <u>reservation</u> have the same meaning as it does in the sentence above?

A A <u>reservation</u> is required in many of the city's best restaurants.

B The pilot had a <u>reservation</u> about flying in such bad weather.

C The <u>reservation</u> was located in a remote part of the state.

D There is a <u>reservation</u> in the will that does not allow the house to be sold.

8 <u>Hazardous</u> means the same as—

F inflammable.

G incorrect.

H unpredictable.

J dangerous.

9 The word <u>originate</u> means—

A irrigate.

B bring into being.

C develop fully.

D reproduce.

10 What is the meaning of the word <u>insulated</u>?

_____
_____
_____
_____

Activity 15 Language: The Second Industrial Revolution

Directions: Niki is writing a summary of what she has discovered about the development of the nation's railroads after the Civil War. Here is a rough draft of the first part of Niki's summary. Darken the circle for the correct answer, or write your answer in the space provided.

>   Before the Civil War, the railroad system in the United States was never yet fully
> **(1)**
> developed. Those rail lines that existed were short, averaging about 100 miles long.
> **(2)**
> There were no direct lines for people who planned to traveling from state to state.
> **(3)**
> Passengers had to change trains frequently this was tiring and time consuming
> **(4)**
> for all.
>
>   But the railways were about to make a major advance. With the availability of
> **(5)**   **(6)**
> cheaper steel. Companies were able to lay track rapidly, thereby expanding their lines.
> **(7)**
> Between 1860 and 1869, major improvements have been made. By 1869, the country
> **(8)**   **(9)**
> had its first transcontinental railroad. The Central Pacific and the Union Pacific
> **(10)**
> Railroads were joined, forming one continuous railroad line from Omaha, Nebraska,
>
> to the Pacific Ocean. By celebrating this historic occasion, the railways now truly
> **(11)**
> served the nation's people.
>
>   By 1900, further advances had been made. Trunk lines which were major
> **(12)**   **(13)**
> railroads ran from the Great Plains to the Pacific coast. A system of shorter lines
> **(14)**
> connected these trunk lines to less accessible regions.

38

NAME _____ CLASS _____ DATE _____

1 What is the best way to rewrite sentence 1?
_____
_____
_____

2 In sentence 3, <u>people who planned to traveling</u> is best written—

   A people who have traveled

   B people who have planned to travel

   C people who planned to travel

   D As it is written.

3 Which sentence in paragraph 1 is a run-on sentence?

   F 1

   G 2

   H 3

   J 4

4 Which group of words in paragraph 2 is not a whole sentence?

   A 5

   B 6

   C 7

   D 8

5 In sentence 8, <u>major improvements have been made</u> is best written—

   F major improvements were being made

   G major improvements would be made

   H major improvements had been made

   J As it is written.

6 How could sentences 8 and 9 be combined without losing the original meaning of either sentence?
_____
_____
_____
_____
_____

7 How is sentence 11 best written?

   A This was an historic occasion to celebrate, as the railways now truly served the nation's people.

   B Celebrating this historic occasion, the railways now truly served the nation's people.

   C The railways now truly served the nation's people, who celebrated.

   D As it is written.

8 In sentence 13, <u>Trunk lines which were major railroads</u> is best punctuated—

   F Trunk lines which, were major railroads

   G Trunk lines, which were major railroads,

   H Trunk lines which, were major railroads,

   J As it is written.

9 What would be a good concluding sentence to Niki's summary?

   A In less than fifty years, many people would own automobiles.

   B The Civil War had delayed the construction of the transcontinental railroad.

   C Now passengers could travel conveniently from large cities to small towns.

   D Of course, some passengers still complained about having to transfer from one train to another.

1 Open-ended   3 Ⓕ Ⓖ Ⓗ Ⓙ   5 Ⓕ Ⓖ Ⓗ Ⓙ   7 Ⓐ Ⓑ Ⓒ Ⓓ   9 Ⓐ Ⓑ Ⓒ Ⓓ
2 Ⓐ Ⓑ Ⓒ Ⓓ   4 Ⓐ Ⓑ Ⓒ Ⓓ   6 Open-ended   8 Ⓕ Ⓖ Ⓗ Ⓙ

NAME _____ CLASS _____ DATE _____

Activity 16 Social Science: The Transformation of American Society

Directions: Darken the circle for the correct answer, or write your answer in the space provided.

1. The term "old immigrants" refers mainly to—
   - A Irish Catholics.
   - B people from southern or eastern Europe.
   - C Protestants from northwestern Europe.
   - D elderly people who endured the hardships of immigration.

2. Most Jewish and Armenian immigrants came to America in order to—
   - F escape religious or political persecution.
   - G seek economic opportunities lacking in their native lands.
   - H earn money and then return to Europe.
   - J work on the nation's expanding railway system.

3. What was the procedure for screening immigrants?
   _____
   _____
   _____
   _____

4. The majority of "new" immigrants settled in—
   - A rural communities throughout the country.
   - B crowded urban areas.
   - C Midwestern farming regions.
   - D states in the Upper South.

5. The Chinese Exclusion Act of 1882 was the result of—
   - F the need for Chinese labor on the railroads.
   - G the Chinese government's decision to limit emigration.
   - H criminal activities committed by Chinese mobs.
   - J the nativist movement in the United States.

6. Between 1865 and 1900, the percentage of urban Americans—
   - A doubled.
   - B tripled.
   - C declined.
   - D remained constant.

7. The growth of suburban areas was encouraged by—
   - F the overcrowding of urban areas.
   - G the political leaders of major cities.
   - H the development of mass transit systems.
   - J the rise of the nouveau riche.

8. The growth of new industries in the late 1800s had little or no effect upon—
   - A the number of middle-class city dwellers.
   - B the relative wages of the working poor.
   - C the rise in the number of professional schools.
   - D the number of women employed outside the home.

1 Ⓐ Ⓑ Ⓒ Ⓓ   3 Open-ended   5 Ⓕ Ⓖ Ⓗ Ⓙ   7 Ⓕ Ⓖ Ⓗ Ⓙ
2 Ⓕ Ⓖ Ⓗ Ⓙ   4 Ⓐ Ⓑ Ⓒ Ⓓ   6 Ⓐ Ⓑ Ⓒ Ⓓ   8 Ⓐ Ⓑ Ⓒ Ⓓ

NAME _____ CLASS _____ DATE _____

9 **According to the map, where did the majority of German immigrants live in 1910?**

 F the West Side of Manhattan
 G along the Hudson River
 H the Bronx
 J the East Side of Manhattan

10 **What were some of the goals of reformers such as Jane Addams?**

_____
_____
_____
_____
_____
_____

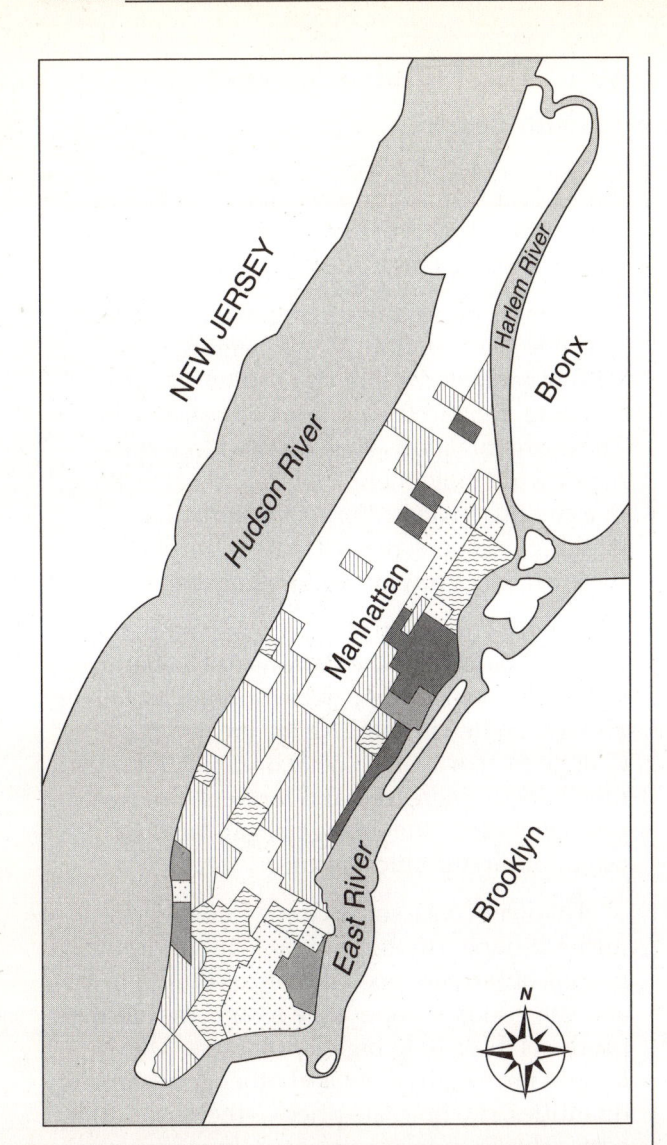

LEGEND:

Manhattan residents of foreign origin, 1910
(shading indicates at least 20% of population)

- Irish
- Italian
- Austrian
- Russian
- German

9 Ⓕ Ⓖ Ⓗ Ⓙ
10 Open-ended

Activity 17 Reading Comprehension: The Populist Movement

Directions: Darken the circle for the correct answer, or write your answer in the space provided.

The Farmer's Plight

In addition to transforming urban life, the surge in industrialization during the late 1800s changed farmers' lives significantly. The rapidly growing population in the urban centers had to be fed. Farmers responded by raising more crops and animals each year. Unfortunately for Americans, farmers in other nations did the same. Prices soon tumbled as supply exceeded demand. At the same time, farm costs, such as railroad freight charges and the price of new machinery, continued to rise. As farm profits plunged, many farmers bought more land and increased production. This greater production pushed prices even lower.

To make matters worse, most farm families had borrowed money to pay for their land or to buy new equipment. They often put their farms up as security for loans. Those who could not repay the loans lost their farms. Many ended up as tenant farmers. Others were forced to become farm laborers. One Minnesota farmer expressed the bitterness felt by many farmers.

> "I settled on this land in good faith; built house and barn, broken up part of the land. Spent years of hard labor grubbing [digging], fencing, and improving. Are they going to drive us out like trespassers?"

To farmers, the situation seemed terribly unfair. The merchants who sold farm equipment were making money. Also prospering were the bankers who lent farmers money and the railroads that hauled the farmers' grain and livestock to market. All that the farmers had to show for their long days of backbreaking labor were rising debts. One farmer wrote, "The railroads have never been so prosperous... The banks have never done a better . . . business . . . And yet agriculture languishes."

Farmers began organizing in an attempt to improve the situation. Many farmers joined local organizations that were committed to assisting them in their day-to-day struggles. These organizations soon merged to form a nationwide movement. Helping to better their lives by provoking reforms in railroad and banking practices, many farmers supported these rapidly growing national organizations.

The first major farmers' organization, the National Grange of the Patrons of Husbandry, or the National Grange, was founded by Oliver Hudson Kelley in 1867. Kelley created the Grange primarily as a social organization. As membership increased and farmers' financial problems grew, the Grange began tackling economic and political issues.

To lower costs, some Grange members formed cooperatives, or organizations, in which groups of farmers pooled their resources to buy and sell goods. Cooperative members sold their products directly to big-city markets. They bought farm equipment and other goods in large quantities at wholesale prices—thereby cutting costs. The Grange's main focus, however, was on forcing states to regulate railroad freight and grain-storage rates. In the early 1870s state legislatures began to respond to pressure from farmers. Illinois, Minnesota, and Wisconsin passed "Granger laws" that created state commissions to standardize such rates.

---

1 The phrase "supply exceeded demand" refers to—

  A a shortage of edible crops.

  B rising farm costs.

  C production by farmers that exceeded public consumption.

  D a drop in prices for farm produce.

2 Why did many farm families lose their land?

_____

_____

_____

_____

_____

1 Ⓐ Ⓑ Ⓒ Ⓓ
2 Open-ended

3 In the late 1800s, farmers expected that the surge in America's urban populations would—

F ruin the economy of agricultural regions.

G soon taper off and reach normal numbers.

H lead to increased agricultural trade with other nations.

J give them a larger market and increased profits.

4 According to the passage, farmers resented the railroads because—

A freight trains did not make frequent stops in agricultural areas of the nation.

B charges for hauling farm produce kept rising.

C railroad companies often bought out bankrupt farmers.

D railroad officials were usually corrupt and dishonest.

5 In this passage, what does the word <u>languishes</u> mean?

F prospers

G borrows

H mourns

J declines

6 The Minnesota farmer quoted in the passage probably blamed—

A the banks and the railroads.

B his more prosperous neighbors.

C the federal government.

D city dwellers.

7 What did farmers hope to accomplish by joining local organizations?

F They hoped to find a wider market for their produce.

G They hoped to force banks and railroads to make reforms.

H They hoped to elect officials who were sympathetic to agriculture.

J They hoped to revolutionize methods of farming.

8 By selling directly to big-city markets, cooperatives could—

A find more consumers of their goods.

B eliminate the need to ship freight by railroad.

C avoid competition with local farmers.

D avoid dealing with distributors and therefore save money.

9 The greatest impact of the Grange Movement was on—

F the standardization of railroad freight and grain-storage rates.

G the interest rates of local lending institutions.

H international trade.

J the growth rate of urban populations.

10 What were the main problems of farmers in the late 1800s?

_____
_____
_____
_____
_____

Activity 18 Reading Vocabulary: The Age of Reform

Directions: Darken the circle for the correct answer, or write your answer in the space provided.

1. > Politics became increasingly <u>corrupt</u> as leaders sought financial gains.

   In which sentence does <u>corrupt</u> have the same meaning as it does in the sentence above?

   A The publishers apologized for their <u>corrupt</u> version of the novel.

   B The mayor was removed from office because he was proved <u>corrupt</u>.

   C Leaving meat unrefrigerated will <u>corrupt</u> it.

   D One dishonest employee can <u>corrupt</u> a company's reputation.

2. What is the meaning of the word <u>progressive</u>?

   _____
   _____
   _____

3. Before the 1900s, women were generally considered <u>subsidiary</u> to men. <u>Subsidiary</u> means—

   F uninformed or ignorant.

   G dull or slow.

   H engaged or married.

   J lower or secondary.

4. Muckrakers commented on the <u>apathy</u> of the public. <u>Apathy</u> means—

   A indifference.

   B enthusiasm.

   C rudeness.

   D tolerance.

5. <u>Premature</u> means—

   F extremely mature or aged.

   G poor or destitute.

   H unexpectedly early.

   J before marriage.

6. <u>Luminous</u> means the same as—

   A generous.

   B laminated.

   C electrical.

   D illuminated.

7. Many women supported the <u>temperance</u> societies founded by reformers. <u>Temperance</u> means—

   F tolerance of all racial groups.

   G reform of social problems.

   H avoidance of alcoholic beverages.

   J vocational training.

NAME _____ CLASS _____ DATE _____

8 <u>Depravity</u> means the same as—

A depression.

B immorality.

C descent.

D illegality.

10 What is the meaning of the word <u>instill</u>?

_____
_____
_____
_____

9 African American and white progressives worked to end racial <u>discrimination</u>.

In which sentence does <u>discrimination</u> have the same meaning as it does in the sentence above?

F Feminists protest economic <u>discrimination</u> against women.

G Chloe's outfits show her good taste and <u>discrimination</u>.

H Choosing films suitable for children requires careful <u>discrimination</u>.

J Employers must make a <u>discrimination</u> between fairness and favoritism.

8 Ⓐ Ⓑ Ⓒ Ⓓ   10 Open-ended
9 Ⓕ Ⓖ Ⓗ Ⓙ

45

Activity 19 Language: Progressive Politicians

Directions: Greg was interested in learning more about Theodore Roosevelt, one of America's most memorable presidents. Here is a rough draft of the first part of Greg's biographical sketch of Theodore Roosevelt. Read the rough draft carefully. Darken the circle for the correct answer, or write your answer in the space provided.

Theodore Roosevelt was one of America's most colorful presidents. He was above
(1)   **(2)**
all an individualist he had two great passions: reading and conservation. Perhaps his
                                                                              (3)
sense of self came from being born from very different parents. His mother a southerner
                                                                         (4)
who sympathized with the Confederates during the Civil War and his father who

believed in the cause of the Union. In one very important respect Roosevelt was a
                                                     (5)
self-made man. As a boy he suffered from asthma, a disease that could have severely
             (6)
limited his future. Young Roosevelt was also nearsighted and physically weak. But
              (7)   **(8)**
through exercise and sheer will power, Roosevelt built himself up into a strong young

man. When Roosevelt finished his term as president, he declared, "I do not believe
       (9)
that anyone else has ever enjoyed the White House as much as I have."

Theodore Roosevelt came to the presidency by accident; he inherited the office after
       (10)
President McKinley was assassinated. The young vice-president had to win over
                                                          (11)
Americans, some of which distrusted his anti-corporate stance and his strong hand in

progressive causes. For instance, he supported the passage of Congressional bills to
                    (12)
regulate the railroads and to restrict the sale of questionable foods and drugs to the public.

Roosevelt also became known as a "trust buster" because he would not allow big
(13)
business a free hand. However, he could also accepted a decent compromise, as he did
                                        (14)
in the case of a major mining strike. Above all, Roosevelt wanted what he called a
                                            (15)
"square deal" for Americans of every social class. He sincerely wanted to help people
                                                       (16)
from all walks of life.

46

1. Which sentence in paragraph 1 is a run-on sentence?
   - A 1
   - B 2
   - C 3
   - D 4

2. How could sentence 3 be rewritten to avoid awkwardness?

   _____
   _____
   _____
   _____

3. Which group of words in paragraph 1 is not a complete sentence?
   - F 2
   - G 3
   - H 4
   - J 5

4. Which sentence would best follow sentence 8?
   - A In 1898 the now-robust Roosevelt became a national hero during the Spanish-American War.
   - B Roosevelt would survive the tragic death of his first wife in 1884.
   - C Roosevelt worked hard to give the United States a prominent position in international affairs.
   - D As a young man, Roosevelt was attracted to a career in public service.

5. Which sentence does not belong in paragraph 1?
   - F 6
   - G 7
   - H 8
   - J 9

6. In sentence 11, *some of which distrusted* is best written—
   - A some of whom distrusted.
   - B some of them distrusted.
   - C some of who distrusted.
   - D As it is written.

7. What is the topic sentence of paragraph 2?
   - F 10
   - G 11
   - H 12
   - J 13

8. In sentence 14, *he could also accepted* is best written—
   - A he could also accept.
   - B he could also have accepted.
   - C he also could accept.
   - D As it is written.

9. Which sentence in paragraph 2 needlessly repeats an idea in a previous sentence?
   - F 13
   - G 14
   - H 15
   - J 16

NAME _____ CLASS _____ DATE _____

Activity 20 Social Science: America and the World

Directions: Darken the circle for the correct answer, or write your answer in the space provided.

1. Industrialized nations attempted to colonize other countries mainly in order to—
   A assert political control over uncolonized nations.
   B find new markets and natural resources.
   C prevent a world war from breaking out.
   D find jobs for Americans abroad.

2.
   > "The ease with which Hawaiians on their own land can secure their food supply has undoubtedly interfered with their social and industrial advancement . . . [It] relieves the native from any struggles and unfits him for sustained competition with men from other lands."
   >
   > From "Expansion in the Pacific" from *An On-Line History of the United States: The Age of Imperialism*, online, September 22, 1999. Copyright © 1996 by Small Planet Communications.
   > Available at:
   > http://www.smplanet.com/imperialism/hawaii.html.
   > Reprinted by permission of the publisher.

   The above quotation from an American visitor to Hawaii is an example of—
   F a scientific study of the Hawaiian people.
   G Americans' openness to cultural diversity.
   H cultural bias and a superior attitude.
   J an accurate and unprejudiced observation.

3. The first U.S. contact with the Hawaiian Islands was made by—
   A Pacific trading and whaling ships.
   B American missionaries in the 1820s.
   C Alfred Thayer Mahan.
   D U.S. officials proposing a treaty in 1875.

4. What took place during the Boxer Rebellion of 1900?
   F Wealthy planters rebelled against Queen Liliuokalani of Hawaii.
   G China was forced to open five ports to Western traders.
   H Japan attacked and defeated China.
   J A group of Chinese nationalists attacked Western missionaries and traders.

5. Critics of U.S. annexation of foreign countries argued that—
   A the United States would bring democracy to the Philippines.
   B commerce was more important than politics.
   C U.S. rule of the Philippines would keep out foreign powers.
   D the United States should not violate the ideals expressed in its own Declaration of Independence.

6. Publisher William Randolph Hearst encouraged U.S. intervention in Cuba because—
   F he believed newspapers should shape public opinion and policy.
   G he was convinced that the Spanish were cruel and brutal colonizers.
   H he was infuriated by the destruction of the *USS Maine* warship.
   J he supported a U.S.-proposed peace plan.

NAME _____ CLASS _____ DATE _____

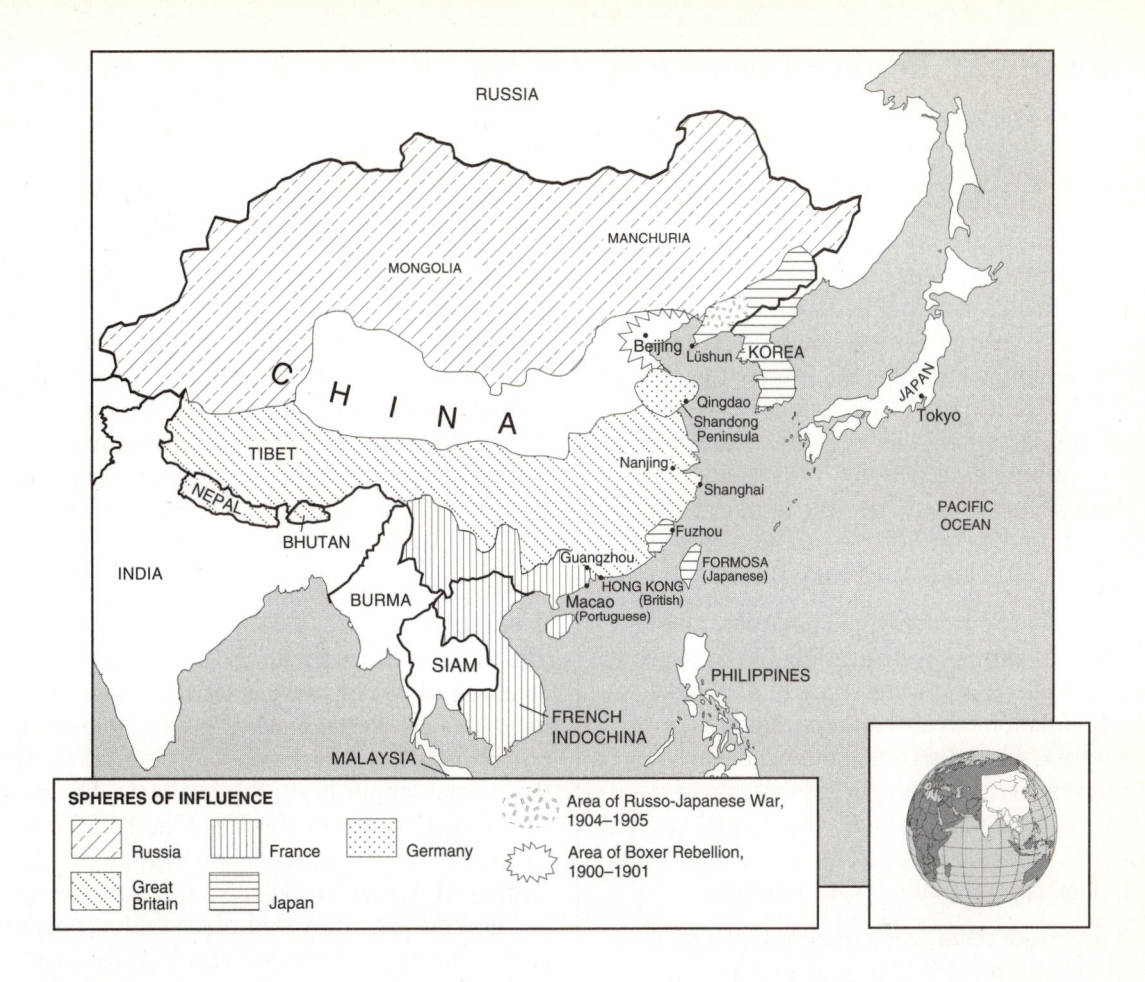

SPHERES OF INFLUENCE
- Russia
- Great Britain
- France
- Japan
- Germany
- Area of Russo-Japanese War, 1904–1905
- Area of Boxer Rebellion, 1900–1901

7 According to the map, which foreign nation controlled the Asian lands closest to Europe?

A Japan

B Russia

C Great Britain

D France

8 A country that is the protectorate of another country—

F must defend that country from military attack.

G receives military protection but gives up some of its political rights.

H is governed wholly by the other country.

J receives political advice from the other country but is not interfered with.

9 As president, Theodore Roosevelt felt it necessary to modify the Monroe Doctrine because—

A he felt the Monroe Doctrine excused excessive territorial aggression.

B he believed the Monroe Doctrine did not allow for U.S. expansion.

C he distrusted people who wished to isolate the United States from other world powers.

D he feared the United States could not protect its own territories.

10 Why have some people described America as an imperialist nation?

_____
_____
_____
_____
_____

7 Ⓐ Ⓑ Ⓒ Ⓓ   9 Ⓐ Ⓑ Ⓒ Ⓓ
8 Ⓕ Ⓖ Ⓗ Ⓙ   10 Open-ended

49

Activity 21 Reading Comprehension: The United States Goes to War

Directions: Darken the circle for the correct answer, or write your answer in the space provided.

U.S. Neutrality

Most Americans were surprised by the outbreak of World War I. However, they tended to look on it as a strictly European matter. President Woodrow Wilson received strong support when he announced a policy of neutrality. He urged all Americans to be "neutral in fact as well as in name . . . impartial in thought as well as action." Wilson hoped that the United States would be able to negotiate a settlement to the conflict. He pursued this goal throughout 1915 and 1916, but without success.

The United States remained neutral in action, but few of its citizens were impartial in thought. Some 28 million Americans—nearly 30 percent of the population—were either immigrants or the children of immigrants. Some Americans of Austrian, German, Hungarian, or Turkish background sympathized with the Central Powers. Some Irish Americans hoped the war would help free Ireland from the rule of Great Britain.

Many more Americans, however, backed the Allies. A common language and culture bound many Americans to Britain. The British propaganda campaign, which painted Germans as brutal killers, also increased American support for the Allies.

Despite its policy of neutrality, the United States could not remain untouched by the war. When the war began, the British navy blockaded Germany and laid mines in the North Sea. The British even stopped U.S. ships bound for neutral countries and searched their cargoes—including the mail. They were looking for goods that might ultimately be destined for Germany. Wilson protested this violation of U.S. neutrality.

Early in 1915 Germany responded to the blockade by establishing a "war zone" around Britain. Any ships entering this zone—even those from neutral nations—were subject to attack by U-boats, or German submarines. Wilson warned that, in accordance with international laws of neutrality, the United States would hold Germany accountable for any injury to American lives or property on the high seas.

On March 28, 1915, a U-boat sank a passenger liner in the Irish Sea, killing more than 100 people, including one American. While the White House considered its response, a far more serious incident occurred. On May 7, 1915, a U-boat patrolling off the Irish coast torpedoed another British passenger liner, the *Lusitania*. The dead included 128 Americans. *The New York Times* called the Germans "savages drunk with blood." Outraged Americans agreed. German leaders pointed out that they had placed advertisements in American newspapers warning Americans against sailing into the war zone. They also charged that the *Lusitania* was transporting armaments for Britain—an accusation that later proved true.

Nevertheless, Wilson protested angrily to the German government. He demanded specific pledges against unrestricted submarine warfare against civilian ships. Secretary of State William Jennings Bryan charged that the president's protest amounted to an ultimatum and resigned. Bryan argued that the United States could not issue ultimatums and remain neutral.

---

1. Any ships entering the German "war zone" were subject to—

   A taxation by the German government.

   B attack by German naval forces.

   C a search by German military police.

   D loss of their neutral status.

2. The event that did most to change America's political stance was—

   F the torpedoing of the *Lusitania*.

   G the resignation of Secretary of State William Jennings Bryan.

   H the death of more than 100 people on a passenger liner.

   J the British blockade of Germany.

3 America was neutral during the early years of World War I because—

A Americans feared an attack by German forces.

B America had a large immigrant population.

C Americans disbelieved British propaganda about Germans.

D American leaders believed Europeans should fight their own war.

4 How did most Americans feel about the political situation at this time?

F supportive of Germany and the other Central Powers

G supportive of the Allies

H completely impartial on the subject of the war

J confused or unclear about their loyalties

5 President Wilson initially believed the role of the United States in the war was that of—

A negotiator.

B military aggressor.

C peacekeeper.

D observer.

6 What is the meaning of the word <u>propaganda</u>?

_____
_____
_____
_____

7 The British stopped American ships bound for neutral countries because—

F the British navy had blockaded the United States.

G the British doubted that the United States would remain neutral.

H the British suspected American ships of carrying goods to the enemy.

J the British navy wanted to seize guns and supplies for their own use.

8 How did Germany defend its attack on the *Lusitania*?

A by reminding Americans they were no longer politically neutral

B by declaring war on the United States

C by denying that German forces were involved in the attack

D by charging that the ship was carrying arms for Britain

9 Why did Secretary of State William Jennings Bryan resign from office?

F He was trying to pressure Wilson into taking a stronger political stance.

G He was sympathetic to the political position of the Central Powers.

H He believed President Wilson had violated his neutrality policy.

J He doubted that Americans would continue to support Wilson's policies.

10 What factors propelled Americans into the war?

_____
_____
_____
_____
_____

---

3 Ⓐ Ⓑ Ⓒ Ⓓ 5 Ⓐ Ⓑ Ⓒ Ⓓ 7 Ⓕ Ⓖ Ⓗ Ⓙ 9 Ⓕ Ⓖ Ⓗ Ⓙ
4 Ⓕ Ⓖ Ⓗ Ⓙ 6 Open-ended 8 Ⓐ Ⓑ Ⓒ Ⓓ 10 Open-ended

NAME _____ CLASS _____ DATE _____

Activity 22 Reading Vocabulary: A Turbulent Decade

Directions: Darken the circle for the correct answer, or write your answer in the space provided.

1. What is the meaning of the word <u>demobilization</u>?

   _____
   _____
   _____

2. "'The same patriotism which <u>induced</u> women to enter industry during the war should induce them to vacate their positions,' declared the New York Labor Federation." <u>Induced</u> means—

   A forced.
   B discouraged.
   C persuaded.
   D allowed.

3. <u>Intimidate</u> means the same as—

   F threaten.
   G intimate.
   H question.
   J strike.

4. > In 1911 American Federation of Labor founder Samuel Gompers decided to <u>recruit</u> John Lewis to organize mine workers.

   In which sentence does <u>recruit</u> have the same meaning as it does in the sentence above?

   A Supplies were quickly used up during times of war, so the military had to frequently <u>recruit</u> more.
   B The new <u>recruit</u> was homesick and lonely.
   C Some colleges strive to <u>recruit</u> students with athletic ability.
   D In a sanitarium, patients rest and <u>recruit</u> their health.

5. <u>Unanimous</u> means—

   F with extreme hostility.
   G having different opinions.
   H sharing the same views.
   J having no particular beliefs.

6. During the Red Scare, several members of the New York State Assembly were <u>expelled</u> because they belonged to the Socialist Party. <u>Expelled</u> means—

   A threatened.
   B dismissed.
   C praised.
   D imprisoned.

7   **Interrogation** means the same as—

F   written evaluation.

G   trial by jury.

H   public denouncement.

J   formal questioning.

8   **What is the meaning of the word incentive?**

_____
_____
_____

9   For years, steel companies tried to suppress workers who attempted to unionize.

In which sentence does suppress have the same meaning as it does in the sentence above?

A   This elixir will suppress even the most persistent cough.

B   The government decided to suppress the committee's final report.

C   Officials at the soccer game had to suppress the riotous behavior of fans.

D   Amnesia victims may be attempting to suppress frightening memories.

10   **Culpable** means—

F   guilty.

G   capable.

H   condemned.

J   innocent.

Activity 23 Language: Henry Ford

Directions: Leah is writing a summary of what she has learned about Henry Ford's influence on the automobile industry. Here is a rough draft of Leah's summary. Read the rough draft carefully. Darken the circle for the correct answer, or write your answer in the space provided.

In the 1920s, the automobile industry in the United States was beginning to
(1)

expand. One man, Henry Ford, did more to advance this growth than any other
(2)

person did to expand this industry. His most significant innovation, the assembly
(3)

line. This new method of production made the manufacturing of automobiles efficient
(4)

and less expensive. This savings was passed along to the consumer. Buyers paid less
(5)   (6)

for their new cars. Today's cars, of course, are far more expensive.
(7)

The new assembly line method did not necessary improve conditions for the
(8)

workers. Doing one job over and over made for boredom, there was no opportunity
(9)

to learn new skills in the assembly line of Ford's factories. Without a secondary
(10)

school degree, a laborer could not hope to obtain a better, more challenging position.

There were also discrimination practices in Ford's workplaces. African Americans
(11)   (12)

were often denied jobs. Probably other minorities were discriminated against, too.
(13)

54

NAME _____ CLASS _____ DATE _____

1. How can sentence 2 be rewritten to avoid unnecessary repetition?

_____
_____
_____

2. Which group of words in paragraph 1 is not a whole sentence?

   A 1
   B 2
   C 3
   D 4

3. Which sentence best follows sentence 4?

   F Ford's new method reduced the time it took to assemble a Model T engine by half.
   G Ford only produced Model Ts in one color: black.
   H The Model T became immensely popular.
   J In the 1920s the automobile industry became the biggest business in the United States.

4. Which sentence in paragraph 1 needlessly repeats an idea expressed in a previous sentence?

   A 3
   B 4
   C 6
   D 7

5. Which sentence does not belong in paragraph 1 of Leah's summary?

   F 4
   G 5
   H 6
   J 7

6. In sentence 8, did not necessary improve is best written—

   A did not necessarily improve
   B did not necessarily improved
   C did not necessary improved
   D As it is written.

7. Which sentence in paragraph 2 is a run-on sentence?

   F 8
   G 9
   H 10
   J 11

8. In sentence 11, discrimination practices is best written—

   A discriminating practices
   B discriminated practices
   C discriminatory practices
   D As it is written.

9. Which sentence in paragraph 2 is not based upon factual information?

   F 9
   G 10
   H 11
   J 13

10. Write an appropriate title for Leah's summary.

_____
_____
_____
_____
_____

1 Open-ended   3 F G H J   5 F G H J   7 F G H J   9 F G H J
2 A B C D   4 A B C D   6 A B C D   8 A B C D   10 Open-ended

55

NAME _____ CLASS _____ DATE _____

Activity 24 Social Science: Prosperity Shattered

Directions: Darken the circle for the correct answer, or write your answer in the space provided.

1. In the 1920s the great increase in consumer spending was a sign of—
   A a crisis in the nation's economic affairs.
   B President Herbert Hoover's popularity.
   C the coming economic depression of the 1930s.
   D the faith of Americans in the nation's economic prosperity.

2. What does the term "bull market" mean?
   F a period of declining stock prices
   G a period of rising stock prices
   H a period of economic panic
   J a period characterized by margin buying

3. The stock market crash of 1929 resulted in—
   A a major banking crisis.
   B a temporary financial panic.
   C the permanent closing of the stock market.
   D an increase in consumer spending based on credit.

4. International economic problems were caused by—
   F America's stock market collapse.
   G an increase in consumer spending in Europe.
   H an increase in international trade.
   J huge war debts owed by European countries.

5. What was one important aim of the Federal Farm Board?
   A to finance the creation of farmers' cooperatives
   B to improve the quality of agricultural products
   C to encourage farmers to produce more crops for consumption
   D to stimulate international trade in farm products

6. Writer Upton Sinclair observed, "The . . . depression is one of abundance, not of scarcity. The cause of the trouble is that a small class has the wealth, while the rest have the debts."

   Upton Sinclair was referring to—
   F overproduction by farmers throughout America.
   G an increase in consumer spending.
   H the gap in income between rich and poor.
   J the rise in salaries of working men and women.

7. By 1933 the jobless figure in the United States was approximately—
   A 1 million.
   B 6 million.
   C 10 million.
   D 15 million.

8. People who had to resort to the breadlines of the 1930s were usually—
   F homeless adults.
   G skilled workers without jobs.
   H orphaned children.
   J unskilled workers.

56   1 Ⓐ Ⓑ Ⓒ Ⓓ   3 Ⓐ Ⓑ Ⓒ Ⓓ   5 Ⓐ Ⓑ Ⓒ Ⓓ   7 Ⓐ Ⓑ Ⓒ Ⓓ
      2 Ⓕ Ⓖ Ⓗ Ⓙ   4 Ⓕ Ⓖ Ⓗ Ⓙ   6 Ⓕ Ⓖ Ⓗ Ⓙ   8 Ⓕ Ⓖ Ⓗ Ⓙ

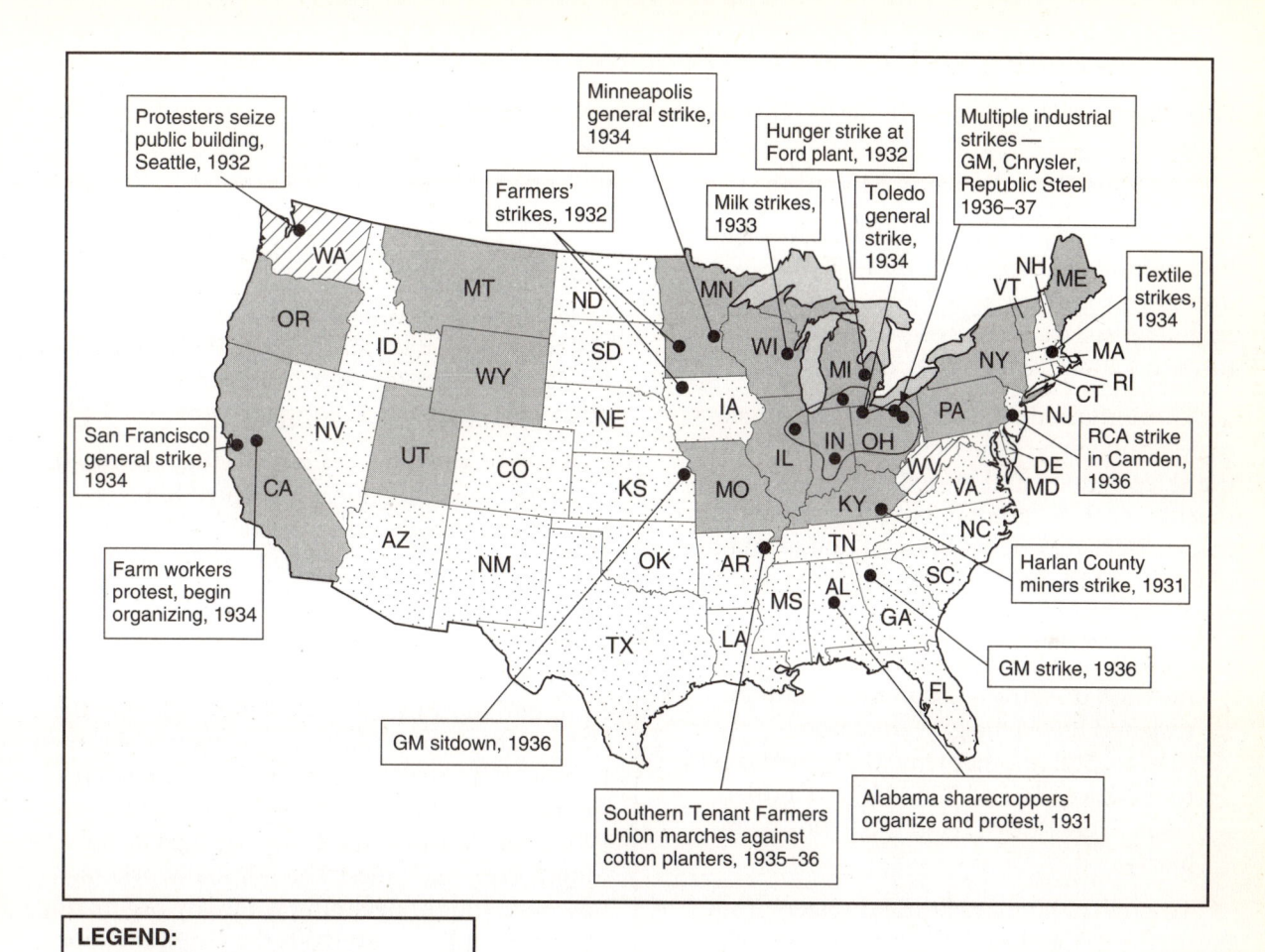

9 According to the map, the greatest concentration of unionized, nonagricultural workers resided in—

A Massachusetts and Rhode Island.

B West Virginia and Washington State.

C Oregon and California.

D New Jersey and Connecticut.

10 What was the main argument against the "trickle down" approach to economic recovery?

NAME _____ CLASS _____ DATE _____

Activity 25 Reading Comprehension: Life in the New Deal Era

Directions: Darken the circle for the correct answer, or write your answer in the space provided.

The Dust Bowl and Migration

The mass migration to California was spurred by a natural disaster. In the mid-1930s a severe drought struck the Great Plains. Winds picked up the topsoil that had loosened and dried, turning a 50-million-acre region into a wasteland.

Throughout the Dust Bowl, as the affected region came to be called, clouds of dust darkened the skies at noon and buried fences and farm machinery. Dust crept into houses through tiny cracks. Ships reported great dust clouds hundreds of miles out to sea. One Texas farmer recalled the drought's effects.

> "If the wind blew one way, here came the dark dust from Oklahoma. Another way and it was the gray dust from Kansas. Still another way, the brown dust from Colorado and New Mexico. Little farms were buried. And the towns were blackened."

To prevent similar natural disasters from occurring in the future, the Department of Agriculture started extensive programs in soil-erosion control. The most dramatic was the planting of some 217 million trees by workers from the Civilian Conservation Corps (CCC). These trees created a windbreak that stretched through the Great Plains from Texas to Canada.

By 1939 the amount of dried-out farmland had decreased dramatically. However, many Dust Bowl farmers had already lost their land. They packed their few belongings into battered old cars or trucks and headed west on Route 66. These migrants saw California and other parts of the West Coast as a Promised Land where they could find work harvesting crops. Since many came from Oklahoma, they were nicknamed "Okies." Once they reached the West Coast they found themselves in fierce competition with other farm laborers looking for work.

Even before the Dust Bowl refugees started arriving, Mexican Americans had a hard time finding work in the West. Like African Americans, Mexican Americans often found themselves the victims of discrimination in many New Deal programs.

Mexican Americans also faced increased job competition from Filipino laborers. During the 1920s California's Filipino population had grown to more than 30,000. Like Mexican American migrants, most Filipinos worked in agriculture. When the depression hit, both groups faced tough economic times. The Filipino workers, however, fought declining wages by organizing. Throughout the early 1930s the Filipino Labor Union launched a series of strikes to protest wage reductions. In 1936 the American Federation of Labor sponsored the Field Workers Union. The union was a combined organization for Mexican American and Filipino laborers.

The unions were able to slow the fall of wages. Yet, with the arrival of additional migrants from the Dust Bowl, competition for jobs increased. Thus, life for all migrants remained difficult.

---

1 The Dust Bowl affected land throughout—
   A Oklahoma.
   B Texas.
   C much of the Great Plains region.
   D the West Coast.

2 What caused the natural disaster described in this passage?
   F loss of trees through disease
   G a severe lack of rainfall
   H the poverty of many migrant workers
   J unemployment among Mexican Americans and Filipinos

NAME _____ CLASS _____ DATE _____

3 The most significant program started by the Department of Agriculture to combat soil erosion involved—

   A planting trees to create windbreaks.
   B creating more jobs for migrant workers.
   C helping Dust Bowl farmers save their land.
   D helping migrants to harvest crops.

4 Many people from the Dust Bowl region relocated to California in order to—

   F obtain work in nonagricultural industries.
   G alert the federal government to their financial problems.
   H buy richer farmland.
   J find work harvesting crops.

5 The quotation from the Texas farmer shows that—

   A Texans were angry with the farmers of neighboring states.
   B dust clouds could travel many hundreds of miles.
   C Texas was the state most affected by the drought.
   D Oklahoma was the center of the Dust Bowl.

6 According to the passage, what major problem did migrant workers arriving in California face?

   F a shortage of affordable housing
   G outbreaks of infectious diseases
   H strikes against unfair employers
   J competition from other farmworkers seeking jobs

7 Filipino workers gained an economic advantage by—

   A accepting low paying jobs in agriculture.
   B competing directly with Mexican American workers.
   C organizing a strong labor union.
   D finding jobs on the East Coast.

8 In this passage, the phrase "wage reductions" means—

   F lowered pay.
   G increase in salary.
   H equal pay.
   J a freeze in hiring for jobs.

9 The unions could not greatly improve life for California's agricultural workers because—

   A state and federal governments fought against the unions.
   B most migrant workers did not wish to join unions.
   C increased job competition meant lower pay for workers.
   D Mexican American and Filipino workers would not join the same unions.

10 How did agricultural workers try to improve their quality of life during this period?

   _____
   _____
   _____
   _____
   _____
   _____

3 Ⓐ Ⓑ Ⓒ Ⓓ   5 Ⓐ Ⓑ Ⓒ Ⓓ   7 Ⓐ Ⓑ Ⓒ Ⓓ   9 Ⓐ Ⓑ Ⓒ Ⓓ
4 Ⓕ Ⓖ Ⓗ Ⓙ   6 Ⓕ Ⓖ Ⓗ Ⓙ   8 Ⓕ Ⓖ Ⓗ Ⓙ   10 Open-ended

NAME _____ CLASS _____ DATE _____

Activity 26 Reading Vocabulary: The Road to War

Directions: Darken the circle for the correct answer, or write your answer in the space provided.

1. After World War I, Germany was required to make substantial war <u>reparations</u>. <u>Reparations</u> mean—

   A repairs to equipment.

   B payments made for damages.

   C changes in federal laws.

   D military trials.

2. What is the meaning of the word <u>isolationism</u>?

   _____
   _____
   _____
   _____

3. <u>Infamous</u> means the same as—

   F related.

   G uncertain.

   H famous.

   J shameful.

4. | Senator William E. Borah argued against membership in the League of Nations, claiming that "The whole scheme has just one <u>ultimate</u> power and that is military force…" |

   In which sentence does <u>ultimate</u> have the same meaning as it does in the sentence above?

   A Our <u>ultimate</u> goal is to prevent another world war from occurring.

   B Germany's political hopes represented the <u>ultimate</u> in world domination.

   C The <u>ultimate</u> decision was to go ahead with the space shuttle launch as planned.

   D Pluto is the <u>ultimate</u> planet in the Milky Way.

5. Certain groups of Americans urged the U.S. government to negotiate <u>disarmament</u> with other world powers. <u>Disarmament</u> means—

   F a peace treaty.

   G a reduction in size of a country's military.

   H a political alliance between two or more nations.

   J an improvement in the quality of weaponry used in war.

NAME _____ CLASS _____ DATE _____

6 <u>Abolish</u> means—
- A to establish.
- B to join.
- C to do away with.
- D to vote against.

7 <u>Potency</u> means the same as—
- F power.
- G condition.
- H potential.
- J age.

8
> The treaty guaranteed China's territorial <u>integrity</u> and required its signers to uphold the Open Door Policy.

In which sentence does <u>integrity</u> have the same meaning as it does in the sentence above?
- A The senator is a person of the greatest <u>integrity</u> and honesty.
- B The <u>integrity</u> of the Union was Abraham Lincoln's greatest concern.
- C The <u>integrity</u> of the new skyscraper was based on its massive foundations.
- D The apparent corruption of his colleagues seriously affected his <u>integrity</u>.

9 Although many Americans called for an economic boycott of Japan, U.S. leaders refused to support <u>sanctions</u> against the Japanese. In this sentence, <u>sanctions</u> mean—
- F insults.
- G considerations.
- H permits.
- J penalties.

10 What is the meaning of the word <u>moratorium</u>?

_____
_____
_____
_____

NAME _____ CLASS _____ DATE _____

Activity 27 Language: World War II

Directions: Carolyn is planning to write a report on what Winston Churchill called the "Battle of Britain." Here is a rough draft of the first part of Carolyn's report. Read the rough draft carefully. Darken the circle for the correct answer, or write your answer in the space provided.

The Battle of Britain

In 1940 a year before the United States joined the Allies to fight the Axis Powers
(1)
Britain was preparing for intense battle with Germany. British Prime Minister
(2)
Winston Churchill probably did not know it. But Churchill made a historical
(3)
pronouncement when he said, "The Battle of Britain is about to begin . . . . The
(4)
whole fury of the enemy must very soon be turned upon us. Hitler knows he must
(5)
break us in this island or lose the war . . ." He also discussed how the United States
(6)
would be in jeopardy without Britain's courageous stand. The British were true
(7)
impressed by their Prime Minister's words. Only one week later. Approximately
(8)   **(9)**
2,650,000 British men were ready to fight Hitler's forces. In addition to the home
(10)
troops, the Battle of Britain was fought by Canadians and Australians.

The British were bombarded throughout that year the Nazis initially targeted
(11)
British airfields, aircraft factories, docks, and oil stores. The British were encouraged
(12)
to feel angry, not frightened, of the bombing attacks. Yet, their leaders did not
(13)
ignore the danger to the civilian population. While soldiers battling the air attacks
(14)
with their own aircraft, thousands of children were sent out of the most dangerous

areas, to temporary homes.

From "Their Finest Hour," speech delivered to the House of Commons, June 18, 1940, by Winston Churchill from *Blood, Sweat, and Tears* by The Right Honorable Winston S. Churchill. Copyright 1941 by Winston S. Churchill. Reprinted by permission of The Putnam Publishing Group.

NAME _____ CLASS _____ DATE _____

1 In paragraph 1, <u>a year before the United States joined the Allies to fight the Axis Powers</u> is best written—

A , a year before the United States joined the Allies to fight the Axis Powers,

B a year, before the United States joined the Allies to fight the Axis Powers

C a year before, the United States joined the Allies to fight the Axis Powers,

D As it is written.

2 How could sentences 2 and 3 best be combined?

_____
_____
_____
_____
_____

3 Which sentence does not belong in paragraph 1?

F 1
G 3
H 6
J 9

4 Which group of words in paragraph 1 is not a whole sentence?

A 5
B 6
C 7
D 8

5 In sentence 7, <u>were true impressed</u> is best written—

F were truly impressed.
G were impressed truthfully.
H were truthfully impressed.
J As it is written.

6 Sentence 10 is best written—

A In the Battle of Britain, Canadians and Australians fought in addition to the home troops.

B In addition to the home troops, Canadians and Australians fought in the Battle of Britain.

C Canadians and Australians in addition to the home troops fought the Battle of Britain.

D As it is written.

7 Which sentence in paragraph 2 is a run-on sentence?

F 11
G 12
H 13
J 14

8 In sentence 14, <u>While soldiers battling the air attacks</u> is best written—

A While soldiers had battled the air attacks.

B While soldiers battle the air attacks.

C While soldiers battled the air attacks.

D As it is written.

9 Which sentence best follows sentence 11?

F British soldiers were instructed to shoot down German parachute troops.

G Later, the Axis Powers began bombing residential areas as well.

H The French Republic was already under the control of the Axis forces.

J Few Germans were shot down in the opening days of the war.

1 Ⓐ Ⓑ Ⓒ Ⓓ   3 Ⓕ Ⓖ Ⓗ Ⓙ   5 Ⓕ Ⓖ Ⓗ Ⓙ   7 Ⓕ Ⓖ Ⓗ Ⓙ   9 Ⓕ Ⓖ Ⓗ Ⓙ
2 Open-ended   4 Ⓐ Ⓑ Ⓒ Ⓓ   6 Ⓐ Ⓑ Ⓒ Ⓓ   8 Ⓐ Ⓑ Ⓒ Ⓓ

NAME _____ CLASS _____ DATE _____

Activity 28 Social Science: The Cold War

Directions: Darken the circle for the correct answer, or write your answer in the space provided.

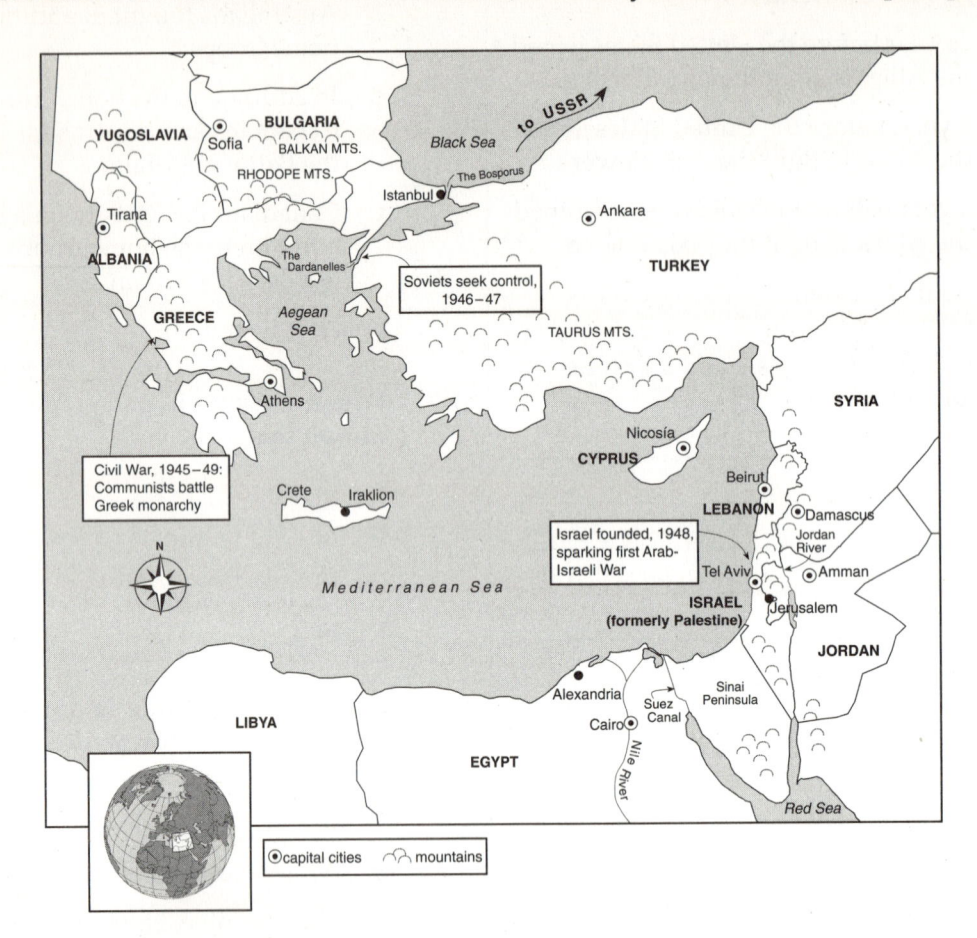

1. **Which international organization was created after World War II with the goal of keeping peace?**

   A the League of Nations
   B the Potsdam Conference
   C the International Military Tribunal for the Far East
   D the United Nations

2. **The purpose of the Nuremberg Trials was to—**

   F punish Hitler for starting World War II.
   G bring Nazi war criminals to trial.
   H conduct trials of war criminals in the Far East.
   J divide Germany into two political zones.

3. **According to the map, which event created tensions in the Middle East?**

   A the battle between Communists and the Greek monarchy
   B attempted Soviet domination of the Balkans
   C the founding of the state of Israel
   D Soviet intervention in the Arab states

4. **Which nation was not a permanent member of the United Nations Security Council?**

   F the Soviet Union
   G France
   H the United States
   J Japan

5. The person most directly responsible for the founding of Israel was—

A Zionist David Ben-Gurion.

B U.S. diplomat Ralph Bunche.

C U.S. president Franklin D. Roosevelt

D British prime minister Winston Churchill.

6. The term "Cold War" refers to—

F the period immediately before the outbreak of World War II.

G the struggle between the United States and the Soviets for political dominance.

H tensions between Japan and China.

J Soviet control of the Baltic states.

7. The U.S. policy of containment was aimed at—

A ending U.S. involvement in foreign wars.

B reducing Arab-Israeli tensions.

C limiting the spread of communism throughout the world.

D halting the arms buildup by world powers.

8. The "Marshall Plan" was another name for—

F the plan to partition the state of Israel.

G the U.S. program to rebuild Japan.

H the recently-founded United Nations.

J the European Recovery Program.

9. The purpose of the North Atlantic Treaty Organization is to—

A protect the member nations from foreign attack.

B give economic aid to member nations.

C keep peace in the Middle East.

D promote trade between European countries.

10. Why did China become a focus of Cold War tensions?

_____
_____
_____
_____
_____

Activity 29 Reading Comprehension: The Challenges of Peace

Directions: Darken the circle for the correct answer, or write your answer in the space provided.

The Problems of Demobilization

By mid-1946 more than 9 million men and women had been discharged from the military. The soldiers received a hero's welcome, but their return also sparked concern. How could the economy absorb all these new workers? Many Americans feared that the country would fall into an economic decline similar to the one that had followed World War I.

Even before the war had ended, Congress began preparing for peace. Preventing an economic depression and helping war-weary veterans make the difficult transition to civilian life were top priorities. Congress passed the Servicemen's Readjustment Act of 1944, more commonly known as the GI Bill of Rights. The bill provided pensions and government loans to help veterans start businesses and buy homes or farms. Millions of veterans also received money through the GI Bill to attend college. Between 1944 and 1962 almost 8 million veterans attended college or technical schools on the GI Bill. This led to a dramatic increase in the number of American college graduates. Government worker Nelson Poynter described the impact of the GI Bill.

"The GI Bill . . . had more to do with thrusting us into a new era than anything else. Millions of people whose parents or grandparents had never dreamed of going to college saw that they could go. . . Essentially I think it made us a far more democratic people." [1]

To ensure postwar economic growth, Congress passed the Employment Act of 1946. The act committed the government to promoting full employment and production. It also established the Council of Economic Advisers to confer with the president on economic policy.

Despite widespread fears, the postwar depression never came. For example, the government canceled some $23 billion in military contracts. Those plants that had been making tanks and bombers began producing consumer goods instead. Employment levels remained high. Many Americans also began to spend the money they had saved during the war. Furthermore, because agricultural output in foreign countries had been shattered by the war, U.S. food exports increased.

Not all was rosy on the economic front, however. Government measures encouraged employers to give priority to veterans in hiring. As a result, many workers lost their jobs to returning veterans. Congress abolished the Fair Employment Practices Committee, which had helped protect African Americans from discrimination. The government also retired the character of "Rosie the Riveter." Instead, the government started a campaign to encourage women to quit their jobs and become full-time homemakers. Some women wanted to keep their jobs. This was particularly true for working-class women whose families needed their incomes. Most women who did not willingly give up their jobs were fired or pressured to quit their jobs after the war.

Another problem that concerned workers was the effect of postwar inflation. The cost of goods soared after most wartime price controls were lifted in 1946. Meat prices zoomed so high that some markets began selling horsemeat. Blaming President Truman, angry consumers called him "Horsemeat Harry."

[1] Quote by Nelson Poynter from *Americans Remember the Home Front: an Oral Narrative of the World War II Years in America* by Roy Hoopes. Published by Berkley Books, New York, 1992.

---

1 According to the selection, when people begin to spend money more freely—

   A the economy is strengthened.

   B a period of economic decline usually follows.

   C manufacturers cannot produce enough goods to satisfy the demand.

   D there is increased competition for jobs.

2 What is one important way Congress began preparing for peacetime?

_____

_____

_____

_____

---

1 Ⓐ Ⓑ Ⓒ Ⓓ

2 Open-ended

NAME _____ CLASS _____ DATE _____

3 **Why did one government worker claim, "The GI Bill . . . had more to do with thrusting us into a new era than anything else"?**

    F The GI Bill allowed many more people to attend college to prepare themselves for better careers.

    G The GI Bill was the first piece of government legislation to ensure equal opportunity for people of all races.

    H The GI Bill allowed women to keep their jobs in factories and offices.

    J The GI Bill prevented returning veterans from taking over jobs from civilians.

4 **When the government canceled approximately $23 billion in military contracts, industry responded by—**

    A going into an economic decline.

    B firing thousands of workers daily.

    C calling emergency meetings with Congress and the president.

    D manufacturing more consumer goods.

5 **An economic cycle characterized by high prices for goods is a period of—**

    F transition.

    G prosperity.

    H depression.

    J inflation.

6 **Why did many Americans fear a postwar economic depression?**

    A American factories could no longer manufacture weapons.

    B Americans were saddened and dispirited by the war.

    C The return of veterans meant increased competition for jobs.

    D An economic depression occured after World War I.

7 **Veterans were able to take over many jobs because—**

    F other people willingly gave up their jobs for the returning heroes.

    G women no longer needed to remain in the workforce.

    H government policies encouraged employers to hire veterans.

    J veterans had acquired many needed skills while serving in the military.

8 **According to the selection, "The government retired the character of 'Rosie the Riveter.'" This means—**

    A a famous American woman retired from government duty.

    B women were no longer encouraged to hold jobs outside the home.

    C working women were no longer portrayed in movies.

    D older women had to retire from their jobs.

9 **Why did U.S. food exports increase in the postwar period?**

    F The war had led to better trade relations between the United States and other nations.

    G Foreign countries had not been able to produce enough food.

    H America needed to obtain food from other countries.

    J American farmers began growing more food crops.

10 **What are three ways in which the GI Bill of Rights improved the quality of life for returning veterans?**

_____

_____

_____

_____

_____

---

3 Ⓕ Ⓖ Ⓗ Ⓙ   5 Ⓕ Ⓖ Ⓗ Ⓙ   7 Ⓕ Ⓖ Ⓗ Ⓙ   9 Ⓕ Ⓖ Ⓗ Ⓙ
4 Ⓐ Ⓑ Ⓒ Ⓓ   6 Ⓐ Ⓑ Ⓒ Ⓓ   8 Ⓐ Ⓑ Ⓒ Ⓓ   10 Open-ended

Activity 30 Reading Vocabulary: The New Frontier and the Great Society

Directions: Darken the circle for the correct answer, or write your answer in the space provided.

1. > At home, Eisenhower shifted <u>domestic</u> policy from the New Deal and the Fair Deal to Modern Republicanism.

   In which sentence does <u>domestic</u> have the same meaning as it does in the sentence above?

   A <u>Domestic</u> animals such as cats and dogs depend upon human beings.

   B Last year, Congress focused on <u>domestic</u> issues rather than on foreign affairs.

   C In <u>domestic</u> science classes, students learn to cook and sew.

   D My mother is a <u>domestic</u> woman; she enjoys managing our home.

2. John Kennedy's statements about the separation of church and state, along with the refusal of Republicans to <u>exploit</u> the issue of religion, reassured voters. <u>Exploit</u> means—

   F make use of for selfish purposes.

   G discuss in an open forum.

   H ignore or avoid an issue.

   J foretell the results of an action.

3. <u>Predecessor</u> means—

   A one who follows.

   B one who is no longer living.

   C one who makes predictions.

   D one who comes before.

4. Latin American countries have often been oppressed by <u>oligarchic</u> governments. <u>Oligarchic</u> means—

   F governments of a democratic character.

   G governments ruled by monarchs.

   H governments ruled by a few people.

   J governments partly ruled by a parliament or other assembly.

5. <u>Incompetent</u> means the same as—

   A incapable.

   B imprecise.

   C unintelligent.

   D unaware.

6. <u>Intimidate</u> means—

   F suggest.

   G threaten.

   H assure.

   J instigate.

NAME _____ CLASS _____ DATE _____

7 The Soviets <u>complied</u> with Castro's request for defensive weapons. <u>Complied</u> means—

   A ignored or disregarded.

   B disagreed or disliked.

   C discussed or debated.

   D agreed or cooperated.

8
> To end <u>speculation</u> about Kennedy's assassination, the Warren Commission studied the evidence relating to the crime.

In which sentence does <u>speculation</u> have the same meaning as it does in the sentence above?

   F The judge's <u>speculation</u> was the result of much thought and study.

   G Financial <u>speculation</u> can be quite risky.

   H Whether the senator will run for office again is a matter of intense <u>speculation</u>.

   J The monks devote themselves to <u>speculation</u> and religious duties.

9 <u>Inevitable</u> means the same as—

   A unavoidable.

   B preventable.

   C predictable.

   D invisible.

10 What does the word <u>charisma</u> mean?

_____
_____
_____
_____

---

7 Ⓐ Ⓑ Ⓒ Ⓓ   **9** Ⓐ Ⓑ Ⓒ Ⓓ

8 Ⓕ Ⓖ Ⓗ Ⓙ   **10** Open-ended

Activity 31 Language: Martin Luther King Jr. and the Civil Rights Movement

Directions: James is interested in the life and activities of Martin Luther King Jr. He is planning to write a report about the famous civil rights leader. Here is a rough draft of the first part of James's report. Read the rough draft carefully. Darken the circle for the correct answer, or write your answer in the space provided.

Martin Luther King Jr.

Some people venerated him. Some people took advantage of him. Others which
(1)   (2)   (3)
were more radical than King scorned him as too "soft" in his message. But even now.
                                                                                                                                    (4)
Over thirty years after his murder, Martin Luther King is remembered by many as
(5)
the most powerful figure in the civil rights movement of the 1960s.

Born on January 15, 1929, Martin Luther King came from a Georgia family known
(6)
for becoming involved in civil rights causes. In college, King decided upon a career
                                                                            (7)
in the ministry. Later, he attended Crozer Theological Seminary, where he read the
                  (8)
works of philosophers and leaders such as Mohandas K. Gandhi. Gandhi was the
                                                                                                            (9)
greatest single influence on young King. The Indian leader's ideas impressed him
                                                                  (10)
deeply. Gandhi's philosophy of nonviolent resistance would become what King
              (11)
describes as his "operational technique." King's first real act in the civil rights
                                                        (12)
movement was his protest for Rosa Parks, the African American woman who

would not give up her bus seat to a white person. I agree with Ms. Parks that she
                                                                                                (13)
should have kept her seat and her dignity. King and his followers won their battle
                                                                                (14)
against the Montgomery bus line, their case came before the U.S. Supreme Court.

70

NAME _____ CLASS _____ DATE _____

1. Which group of words in paragraph 1 is not a whole sentence?

   A 1
   B 2
   C 3
   D 4

2. In sentence 3, <u>which were more radical</u> is best written—

   F while were more radical.
   G who were more radical.
   H that was more radical.
   J As it is written.

3. Combine sentences 4 and 5 and rewrite them to avoid awkward sentence structure.

   _____
   _____
   _____
   _____

4. Which sentence in paragraph 2 needlessly repeats an idea stated in a previous sentence?

   A 10
   B 11
   C 12
   D 13

5. In sentence 12, <u>his protest for Rosa Parks</u> is best written—

   F his protest against Rosa Parks.
   G his protest in favor of Rosa Parks.
   H his protest on behalf of Rosa Parks.
   J As it is written.

6. Which sentence does not belong in paragraph 2?

   A 11
   B 12
   C 13
   D 14

7. Which sentence in paragraph 2 is a run-on sentence?

   F 6
   G 8
   H 11
   J 14

8. At what point should James begin a new paragraph?

   A after sentence 10
   B after sentence 11
   C after sentence 12
   D after sentence 13

1 Ⓐ Ⓑ Ⓒ Ⓓ   3 Open-ended   5 Ⓕ Ⓖ Ⓗ Ⓙ   7 Ⓕ Ⓖ Ⓗ Ⓙ
2 Ⓕ Ⓖ Ⓗ Ⓙ   4 Ⓐ Ⓑ Ⓒ Ⓓ   6 Ⓐ Ⓑ Ⓒ Ⓓ   8 Ⓐ Ⓑ Ⓒ Ⓓ

Activity 32 Social Science: Struggles for Change

Directions: Darken the circle for the correct answer, or write your answer in the space provided.

1. Betty Friedan's groundbreaking book, *The Feminine Mystique*, revealed that many women of the 1960s—

    A had little or no higher education.

    B were most concerned with marriage and child-rearing.

    C were engaged in fair economic competition with men.

    D were dissatisfied with their roles as homemakers.

2. The Supreme Court decision in the case *Roe* v. *Wade* meant that—

    F abortion now would be illegal throughout the United States.

    G women could have legal abortions during the first trimester of pregnancy.

    H discrimination on the basis of sex would be illegal.

    J no person could be denied educational opportunity on the basis of sex or race.

3. César Chávez devoted his life to—

    A helping migrant agricultural workers obtain fair pay.

    B gaining equal rights for African Americans.

    C organizing a labor union for Filipino workers.

    D helping Hispanic women find jobs in agriculture.

4. In what ways did Indian leader Mohandas K. Gandhi influence Martin Luther King Jr. and César Chávez?

    _____
    _____
    _____
    _____
    _____

5. What cause did the organization Alianza Federal de Mercedes represent?

    F It represented migrant workers in northern California.

    G It represented poor Hispanic women who were in need of medical help.

    H It represented African Americans who needed financial assistance.

    J It represented Mexican Americans who had land illegally taken from them.

6. The term "Chicano" refers to—

    A all Hispanics in the United States.

    B radical African American politicians.

    C Mexican Americans throughout the United States.

    D a political party based in New Mexico.

7 Participants in the Red Power movement sought—

   F the right to self-government for American Indians.

   G a separate government for Chinese Americans.

   H peaceful relations between the United States and the Soviet Union.

   J more government intervention on American Indian reservations.

8 What are two ways in which many states began to help disabled people in the 1970s?

   _____
   _____
   _____
   _____

9 The term "generation gap" refers to—

   A the number of people born in various generations.

   B people born during the post-World War II baby boom.

   C the rights and problems of elderly citizens.

   D changes in the values held by people of different ages.

10 Artists who invented the style known as "pop art" were involved in—

   F reintroducing people to artists of the classical period.

   G creating art that would appeal to popular tastes.

   H blending advertising with fine art.

   J creating art that celebrated diverse cultures.

---

7 Ⓕ Ⓖ Ⓗ Ⓙ   9 Ⓐ Ⓑ Ⓒ Ⓓ
8 Open-ended 10 Ⓕ Ⓖ Ⓗ Ⓙ

Activity 33 Reading Comprehension: War in Vietnam

Directions: Darken the circle for the correct answer, or write your answer in the space provided.

The Regime of Ngo Dinh Diem

President Eisenhower hoped that southern Vietnam, at least, might be kept noncommunist. He pinned his hopes on Ngo Dinh Diem (NGOH DIN de-EM). A former government official under the French, Diem was enough of a nationalist to be a credible Vietnam leader.

Diem takes power in the south. Ngo Dinh Diem was strongly anticommunist. He had spent several years in the United States, where his political views attracted powerful backers. In 1955 Diem became president of the newly established Republic of Vietnam, or South Vietnam, in an election that was obviously rigged. In Saigon, for example, Diem received more than 605,000 votes from just 450,000 registered voters. Diem knew that he had no chance of winning a nation-wide election against Ho Chi Minh. Therefore, when the July 1956 date set by the Geneva Conference arrived, Diem refused to call an election in the south.

Diem, a Roman Catholic, was unpopular from the start. The large Buddhist population resented the favoritism he showed the Catholics. Peasants disliked his land policies, which favored wealthy landholders. Almost everyone objected to power being kept solely in the grip of Diem's family. Above all, people feared his ruthless efforts to root out his political enemies. Diem's hated security forces routinely tortured and imprisoned opponents.

By the late 1950s armed revolution had erupted in the south. In 1959 military assistance began flowing from the north to the Vietminh who had stayed in the south. In 1960 the southern Vietminh formed the National Liberation Front (NLF). The NLF's main goal was the overthrow of Diem's regime. Members of this rebel force were called Vietcong, for Vietnamese Communists, by their opponents. Not all NLF supporters, however, were Communists.

Many peasants joined the ranks of the NLF. Some did so because of government repression. Others joined out of fear of the NLF. Like Diem's forces, the NLF used terrorist tactics, assassinating hundreds of government officials. Soon much of the countryside was under Vietcong control.

U.S. involvement deepens. John F. Kennedy, who became president in 1961, fully subscribed to the domino theory. He also was eager to bolster the U.S. image in the world. This image had been tarnished by the failed Bay of Pigs invasion and the building of the Berlin Wall early in his presidency. Aiding South Vietnam provided the United States with a chance to assert its power.

When Kennedy took office, there were some 900 U.S. military advisers in South Vietnam training Diem's Army of the Republic of Vietnam (ARVN). During the next few years, Kennedy increased that number to more than 16,000. As Vietcong attacks mounted, Kennedy authorized U.S. forces to engage in direct combat. As a result, the number of Americans killed or wounded climbed from 14 in 1961 to nearly 500 in 1963.

---

1. Why did Eisenhower want the United States to become involved in Vietnam?

   A to support the candidacy of Ngo Dinh Diem

   B to establish fair elections in southern Vietnam

   C to prevent the communists from controlling southern Vietnam

   D to drive the French out of Vietnam

2. In this selection, the word <u>credible</u> means—

   F believable or reliable.

   G trusting or innocent.

   H strong or inspiring.

   J weak or shaky.

NAME _____ CLASS _____ DATE _____

3 Why was it obvious that the election of 1955 was rigged, or dishonest?

   A The French had only recently given up control of southern Vietnam.

   B Diem and Ho Chi Minh were equally popular leaders.

   C Ngo Dinh Diem won the election.

   D There were more votes than there were voters.

4 In 1956, why did Diem refuse to call an election in the south?

   F He knew he would lose to Ho Chi Minh.

   G He wanted to be sure that the entire country had one central government.

   H He no longer wanted a position in government.

   J He knew there were not enough registered voters in the south.

5 According to the selection, Diem was unpopular mostly because—

   A he had the support of the United States.

   B he insulted the character of Ho Chi Minh.

   C he was brutal toward people who opposed him politically.

   D he was strongly anticommunist.

6 From the information in the selection, you can tell that Diem—

   F was a just and responsible leader.

   G preferred the French to the Americans.

   H struggled to keep northern and southern Vietnam united.

   J was politically influenced by foreign powers.

7 Why did armed revolution erupt in the south of the country?

   A Most southern Vietnamese supported communism.

   B Many people wanted to overthrow President Diem.

   C The United States backed a revolution by the peasants.

   D President Diem called upon the military to drive out the NLF.

8 Who formed the National Liberation Front?

   F northern Vietcong who sought control of southern Vietnam

   G President Diem's military forces

   H southern Vietminh who were against President Diem

   J U.S. military advisers in Southeast Asia

9 Why did U.S. military involvement increase dramatically under Kennedy?

   A Kennedy authorized more U.S. forces to fight the Vietcong.

   B Many more Americans enlisted in the armed forces.

   C President Diem begged for more U.S. support.

   D Kennedy sent in more military advisers to South Vietnam.

10 How did the United States help to provoke and escalate the Vietnam War?

   _____
   _____
   _____
   _____
   _____

NAME _____ CLASS _____ DATE _____

Activity 34 Reading Vocabulary: From Nixon to Carter

Directions: Darken the circle for the correct answer, or write your answer in the space provided.

1. As the war <u>escalated</u>, so did criticism of the U.S. role in the conflict. <u>Escalated</u> means—

   A decreased.
   B intensified.
   C succeeded.
   D erupted.

2. <u>Embargo</u> means—

   F a suspension of trade.
   G a reversal in foreign policy.
   H an inflated economy.
   J an embarrassing situation.

3. The Clean Air Act set tough <u>emissions</u> guidelines for automakers. <u>Emissions</u> mean—

   A products that are manufactured in factories.
   B price controls on manufactured products.
   C matter that is discharged into the air.
   D errors committed on factory assembly lines.

4. <u>Sovereignty</u> means the same as—

   F absolute monarchy.
   G democratic government.
   H military control.
   J political authority.

5. Nixon's friendly relations with China gave him <u>leverage</u> to promote a new policy with the Soviet Union. <u>Leverage</u> means—

   A economic security.
   B power to act effectively.
   C political popularity.
   D guaranteed rights.

6. For over twenty years, relations between China and the United States had been <u>suspended</u>.

   In which sentence does <u>suspended</u> have the same meaning as it does in the sentence above?

   F The Brooklyn Bridge is <u>suspended</u> from strong cables.
   G The student was <u>suspended</u> from school for a period of ten days.
   H The trial was <u>suspended</u> due to a problem with one of the witnesses.
   J The judge gave the convicted man a fine and a <u>suspended</u> sentence.

7 **Mutual** means—

   A having the same relationship to one another.

   B having an economic interest in a foreign country.

   C having power over another person or thing.

   D having friendly relations with another nation.

8 **Infinitely** means the same as—

   F endlessly.

   G impatiently.

   H carefully.

   J knowingly.

9 > After the Six-Day War between Arabs and Israelis, détente survived a critical test, though a lasting peace in the Middle East was in doubt.

   In which sentence does critical have the same meaning as it does in the sentence above?

   A The voters were extremely critical of the senator's record.

   B Our teacher gave a critical reading of Hawthorne's novel.

   C Have you read many critical writings on this author's works?

   D A civil war is always a critical period in a nation's history.

10 What does the word **intervene** mean?

   _____
   _____
   _____
   _____

NAME _____ CLASS _____ DATE _____

Activity 35 Language: Women in the Military

Directions: Valerie wanted to express her opinion on the role of women in the U. S. military. Here is a rough draft of the first part of Valerie's persuasive essay. Read the rough draft carefully. Darken the circle for the correct answer, or write your answer in the space provided.

Women in the Military: The Gulf War

In 1991, the U.S. Senate finally allowed women to serve as combat pilots.
(1)
Why should it have taken so long for the U.S. government to come around? After all,
(2)   **(3)**
women have served in the military in many different roles for years. Yet, even today,
                                                                 (4)
women soldiers are restricted in their role in ground battles. Why should this be
                                                                 (5)
the case? Why should this limitation continue to be imposed?
                    (6)

Men are usually the ones to make such decisions, they insist that a woman's
(7)
slighter build makes them weaker and less fit to confront the enemy directly. Critics
                                                                     (8)
of women as soldiers viewed women as likely to slow down a military unit. This is
                                                                       (9)
creating a problem for other soldiers, they say. Others admit that the new technology
                                          (10)
makes a person's gender unimportant.

The Persian Gulf War did a lot to change how people viewed the efficiency of
(11)
women in combat. Approximately 35,000 women served in Operation Desert Storm;
                    (12)
and brought the nation's attention to their skill and courage. One high-ranking officer,
                                                                     (13)
Air Force colonel Douglas Kennett admitted that women soldiers were necessary

in his branch of the armed services. She helped win the war and that should not
                                                        (14)
be forgotten.

78

NAME _____ CLASS _____ DATE _____

1. Write a topic sentence for Valerie's first paragraph.

   _____
   _____
   _____
   _____

2. Which sentence in paragraph 1 needlessly repeats an idea stated in a previous sentence?

   A 2
   B 3
   C 4
   D 6

3. Which sentence in paragraph 2 is a run-on sentence?

   F 7
   G 8
   H 9
   J 10

4. Which sentence in paragraph 2 contains an unnecessary shift in verb tense?

   A 7
   B 8
   C 9
   D 10

5. In sentence 9, **This is creating** is best written—

   F This created
   G This had created
   H This creates
   J As it is written.

6. Which sentence does not belong in paragraph 2?

   A 7
   B 8
   C 9
   D 10

7. In sentence 12, **Operation Desert Storm; and brought** is best written—

   F Operation Desert Storm, and brought
   G Operation Desert Storm: and brought
   H Operation Desert Storm. And brought
   J As it is written.

8. Sentence 13 is best punctuated—

   A One, high-ranking officer, Air Force colonel Douglas Kennett
   B One high-ranking officer, Air Force colonel Douglas Kennett,
   C One high-ranking officer Air Force colonel Douglas Kennett,
   D As it is written.

9. How is sentence 14 best rewritten to make its pronoun agree with its antecedent, **women soldiers**, in the previous sentence?

   _____
   _____
   _____
   _____
   _____

---

1 Open-ended   3 Ⓕ Ⓖ Ⓗ Ⓙ   5 Ⓕ Ⓖ Ⓗ Ⓙ   7 Ⓕ Ⓖ Ⓗ Ⓙ   9 Open-ended
2 Ⓐ Ⓑ Ⓒ Ⓓ   4 Ⓐ Ⓑ Ⓒ Ⓓ   6 Ⓐ Ⓑ Ⓒ Ⓓ   8 Ⓐ Ⓑ Ⓒ Ⓓ

NAME _____ CLASS _____ DATE _____

Activity 36 Social Science: Life in the 1990s and Beyond

Directions: Darken the circle for the correct answer, or write your answer in the space provided.

1. As a presidential candidate, Bill Clinton focused on—
   A federal regulation.
   B renewal of the nation.
   C strengthening the military.
   D decreasing the influence of political lobbyists.

2. Why was 1992 referred to as "the year of the woman"?
   F Hilary Rodham Clinton became involved in the federal government.
   G Anita Hill gained the nation's attention in Senate hearings.
   H More women entered the workforce than in any other year.
   J There was a marked increase in the number of women running for political office.

3. In his first term of office, Clinton's greatest success involved—
   A winning the support of conservative politicians.
   B reducing the national debt.
   C passing a comprehensive health care bill.
   D helping to attain peace in the Middle East.

4. Why did so many ethnic and local disputes erupt in Eastern Europe?
   F Communist authorities no longer kept these tensions under control.
   G More ethnic peoples moved to countries in Eastern Europe.
   H Communist officials cracked down on Eastern European countries.
   J There was an increase in terrorist activities in this region.

5. What is the meaning of the word <u>apartheid</u>?
   _____
   _____
   _____
   _____

6. The high death toll in Bosnia was the result of—
   A a series of major earthquakes in the area.
   B an epidemic of deadly diseases that swept the region.
   C Serbian efforts to drive Muslims out of Bosnia.
   D armed conflict between Bosnians and UN peacekeeping forces.

1 Ⓐ Ⓑ Ⓒ Ⓓ   3 Ⓐ Ⓑ Ⓒ Ⓓ   5 Open-ended
2 Ⓕ Ⓖ Ⓗ Ⓙ   4 Ⓕ Ⓖ Ⓗ Ⓙ   6 Ⓐ Ⓑ Ⓒ Ⓓ

NAME _____ CLASS _____ DATE _____

7 During the 1990s, a Republican-led Congress tried to—

F implement more social programs throughout the nation.

G reduce inflation in the country.

H improve an unhealthy economy.

J cut popular social and environmental programs.

8 Many Americans became wealthier due to—

A a period of stagflation.

B a booming stock market.

C a change in the tax laws.

D increased confidence in the federal government.

9 The term "Y2K bug" refers to—

F widespread computer failure predicted for the year 2000.

G a deadly epidemic predicted for the year 2000.

H the problem of racial relations in the closing year of the century.

J a period of inflation that may occur with the new century.

10 How has use of the Internet as a marketing tool affected international trade?

_____
_____
_____
_____
_____

7 Ⓕ Ⓖ Ⓗ Ⓙ   9 Ⓕ Ⓖ Ⓗ Ⓙ
8 Ⓐ Ⓑ Ⓒ Ⓓ   10 Open-ended

81

Activity 37 Reading Comprehension: Industrialism and Empire

Directions: Darken the circle for the correct answer, or write your answer in the space provided.

Industrialization and Empire

A variety of motives lay behind the renewed enthusiasm for imperialism. Some people viewed imperialism as a way to spread Christianity. Others claimed that Western culture was superior to other world cultures, and that westerners thus had a duty to spread their culture as far as possible. British poet Rudyard Kipling called this duty "the white man's burden." British imperialist Cecil Rhodes put it bluntly. "We happen to be the best people in the world . . . and the more of the world we inhabit, the better it is for humanity." Even U.S. president Theodore Roosevelt echoed this feeling.

> "Every expansion of a great civilized power means a victory for law, order, and righteousness. This has been the case in every instance of expansion during the present century, whether the expanding power were France or England, Russia or America."

However, many historians believe that industrialization was the primary cause for the renewed interest in imperialism. As countries developed their manufacturing industries, they typically became dependent on foreign countries for raw materials. For example, the imperial powers looked to India and Egypt for cotton and to central Africa and Southeast Asia for rubber. Labor also tended to be cheaper in many Asian and African areas than in Europe. In addition, industrialized nations sought foreign markets to sell their products. China alone had millions of potential consumers of manufactured goods.

Industrialization also helped make the new imperialism possible. Just as railroads had enabled expansion on land, steamships extended imperial power on the seas. Steamships required regular refueling. This meant that imperial powers had to establish numerous coaling stations—ports where ships could restock their supplies of coal—to supply their fleets around the world.

Another major contribution of industrialization to imperialism was modern weaponry, like the Maxim machine gun. English writer Hilaire Belloc summed up the importance of such weapons in a famous couplet. "Whatever happens we have got/The Maxim gun and they have not." Modern weapons made it nearly impossible for the inhabitants of colonized areas to resist Western imperialism. For example, in 1898 a force of Africans armed largely with spears and swords attempted to stop British advances in northeast Africa. The resulting Battle of Omdurman left more than 10,000 Africans dead. Fewer than 50 British soldiers were killed.

---

1. In the selection, the word <u>motives</u> means—

    A   truths.

    B   projects.

    C   fears.

    D   reasons.

2. This selection is mostly about—

    F   the reasons underlying Western imperialism.

    G   the superiority of Western culture.

    H   the rise of Africa and India as world cultures.

    J   the development of transportation in the 1800s.

3 The author quotes Rudyard Kipling and Cecil Rhodes in order to show that—

A Rhodes was greatly influenced by the writings of Kipling.

B white westerners felt themselves superior to people of other backgrounds.

C Kipling and Rhodes supported the politics of U.S. president Theodore Roosevelt.

D many Europeans were resettling in Africa and Asia.

4 According to the selection, how did industrialization link West to East?

F Many Western manufacturers set up companies in the East.

G Asians and Africans needed goods made in the West.

H Western manufacturers needed raw materials found in the East.

J Changes in technology made it easier for people in the East and West to communicate with one another.

5 The quotation from Theodore Roosevelt shows that—

A he feared the long-term effects of imperialism.

B he doubted that European powers could ever defeat the United States.

C he was the first American president to support U.S. expansionism.

D he believed that stronger nations could and should rule weaker countries.

6 Why did imperial powers have to establish many coaling stations around the world?

_____
_____
_____
_____

7 According to this selection, foreign powers—

F brought great wealth to countries in Asia and Africa.

G lost money when they invested in poor, underdeveloped areas.

H saved money on labor when they gained control of foreign countries.

J did not expect to make any profits when they embarked on imperialist ventures.

8 In this selection, <u>potential</u> means—

A possible.

B wealthy.

C needy.

D powerful.

9 What does the couplet written by Hilaire Belloc mean?

F Weaker powers were trying to get advanced weaponry for self-defense.

G Modern weapons made the contest between East and West equal.

H Western powers would defeat weaker nations because of superior weaponry.

J Westerners feared uprisings by colonized peoples in the East.

10 The fate of Africans in the Battle of Omdurman mainly shows that—

A the Africans were united against the British forces.

B the Africans did not understand the effectiveness of modern weaponry.

C British soldiers were afraid of the powerful spear throwers of northeast Africa.

D the Africans would soon accept British rule.

---

3 Ⓐ Ⓑ Ⓒ Ⓓ   5 Ⓐ Ⓑ Ⓒ Ⓓ   7 Ⓕ Ⓖ Ⓗ Ⓙ   9 Ⓕ Ⓖ Ⓗ Ⓙ
4 Ⓕ Ⓖ Ⓗ Ⓙ   6 Open-ended   8 Ⓐ Ⓑ Ⓒ Ⓓ   10 Ⓐ Ⓑ Ⓒ Ⓓ

NAME _____ CLASS _____ DATE _____

Activity 38 Reading Vocabulary: The Rise of the Global Economy

Directions: Darken the circle for the correct answer, or write your answer in the space provided.

1. In 1830, Alexis de Tocqueville noted, "At the present time ... the nations seem to be advancing to <u>unity</u>." Unity means the same as—

   A singleness.

   B disagreement.

   C democracy.

   D government.

2. <u>Vulnerable</u> means—

   F sympathetic to others.

   G of great power.

   H easy to injure.

   J lasting in strength.

3. <u>Compelled</u> is the same as—

   A compromised.

   B forced.

   C caused.

   D allowed.

4. | The Monroe Doctrine stated that any show of an unfriendly <u>disposition</u> by Europe toward the United States would be acted on by the U.S. government. |

   In which sentence does <u>disposition</u> have the same meaning as it does in the sentence above?

   F That country has a <u>disposition</u> to maintain the peace.

   G The lawyer took care of the <u>disposition</u> of his client's wealth.

   H The judge has the <u>disposition</u> to hand down sentences to convicted persons.

   J The child has a sweet and loving <u>disposition</u>.

5. What is the meaning of the word <u>commercialism</u>?

   _____
   _____
   _____
   _____
   _____

1 Ⓐ Ⓑ Ⓒ Ⓓ   3 Ⓐ Ⓑ Ⓒ Ⓓ   5 Open-ended
2 Ⓕ Ⓖ Ⓗ Ⓙ   4 Ⓕ Ⓖ Ⓗ Ⓙ

NAME _____ CLASS _____ DATE _____

6 **Animating** means the same as—
   A lively.
   B animal-like.
   C motivating.
   D increasing.

7 | Advances in transportation and communication lowered the cost of many **staples**. |

   In which sentence does staples have the same meaning as it does in the sentence above?
   F You can fasten those papers using a paper clip or **staples**.
   G Liberty and independence are **staples** of democratic governments.
   H The length and fineness of cotton are called its **staples**.
   J Cotton and rice were **staples** of the southern economy.

8 **Perishable** goods require refrigeration. Something that is **perishable**—
   A costs a lot.
   B spoils quickly.
   C is against the law.
   D is easily broken.

9 **Literally** means—
   F simply.
   G actually.
   H noisily.
   J seemingly.

10 Skyrocketing inflation in Germany left it unable to pay any **reparations**. **Reparations** means—
   A compensation.
   B reductions.
   C apologies.
   D respects.

Activity 39 Language: The Movement of People and Ideas

Directions: Derek wanted to write a personal essay about the role the Internet plays in his life. Here is a rough draft of the first part of Derek's personal essay. Read the rough draft carefully. Darken the circle for the correct answer, or write your answer in the space provided.

The Internet in Daily Life: One Student's View

Only a few years ago I was in the middle of writing a research paper. I had to find
   (1)   (2)

some more facts to include in my research paper. I jumped on my bicycle and
                                                                   (3)

pedaled as fast as I could to the nearest library. Because it was almost closing time
                                                              (4)

at the local branch. I hurried to the encyclopedias in the reference section. I flipped
                  (5)   (6)

through the pages desperately trying to find a few facts before closing time was

announced, breathlessly I scribbled down what I needed and headed out the door.

Whew! I had just made it before the library closed for the day.
(7)   (8)

    Yesterday, I once again found myself collecting information for a school
     (9)

assignment without any trouble. I switched on my computer, entered the basic
                                                  (10)

information, and in less than five minutes had several possible sources at my

fingertips. Shopping on-line is just as easy. I quickly accessed each of these sights,
            (11)   (12)

printing out the pages that I needed. Ten or fifteen minutes later, I was back
                                         (13)

at work on my research paper.

NAME _____ CLASS _____ DATE _____

1 In sentence 1, <u>Only a few years ago</u> is best written—

  A ,Only a few years ago
  B ,Only a few years ago,
  C Only a few years ago,
  D As it is written.

2 How are sentences 1 and 2 best combined to avoid needless repetition?

_____
_____
_____
_____

3 Which group of words is not a whole sentence?

  F 4
  G 5
  H 6
  J 7

4 Which sentence is a run-on sentence?

  A 3
  B 4
  C 5
  D 6

5 Which sentence needlessly repeats an idea stated in a previous sentence?

  F 5
  G 6
  H 7
  J 8

6 How is sentence 9 best rewritten so that the phrase <u>without any trouble</u> is correctly placed?

_____
_____
_____
_____
_____

7 Which sentence does not belong in paragraph 2?

  A 9
  B 10
  C 11
  D 12

8 In sentence 12, <u>sights</u> is best written—

  F cites.
  G sites.
  H sides.
  J As it is written.

9 Which of the following sentences would best follow sentence 13?

  A The speed of the Internet had made my research a snap.
  B Some people doubt that the information on the Internet is accurate.
  C People all over the world have learned to love this wonderful tool.
  D Now I had plenty of time to relax before dinner.

1 Ⓐ Ⓑ Ⓒ Ⓓ   3 Ⓕ Ⓖ Ⓗ Ⓙ   5 Ⓕ Ⓖ Ⓗ Ⓙ   7 Ⓐ Ⓑ Ⓒ Ⓓ   9 Ⓐ Ⓑ Ⓒ Ⓓ
2 Open-ended 4 Ⓐ Ⓑ Ⓒ Ⓓ   6 Open-ended 8 Ⓕ Ⓖ Ⓗ Ⓙ

NAME _____ CLASS _____ DATE _____

Activity 40 Social Science: The Struggle for Human Rights

Directions: Darken the circle for the correct answer, or write your answer in the space provided.

1. How did the American Revolution influence European politics?

   A It influenced the British Parliament to break the absolute power of their monarchy.

   B It influenced the French to overthrow their monarchy.

   C It influenced Englishman John Locke to write about natural rights.

   D It influenced Europeans to abolish the slave trade.

2. In the mid to late 1800s, British warships seized slave ships in order to—

   F transport the slaves to British colonies to do manual labor.

   G reward the captains of these ships for bringing slaves to England.

   H rob the crew of any profits they had made from the slave trade.

   J release enslaved men and women from captivity.

3. American abolitionists in the 1800s were encouraged by the fact that—

   A European and Latin American countries were abolishing slavery.

   B North Americans had been the first people to abolish slavery.

   C southern planters were willing to listen to northern abolitionists.

   D the Declaration of Independence supported equal rights for all people.

> "There is something that Governments care for far more than human life, and that is the security of property. So it is through property that we shall strike the enemy."

4. These words were spoken by Emmeline Pankhurst in order to—

   F encourage Americans to go on strike for fair working conditions.

   G warn women suffragists that the government would shoot them if they protested unfair laws.

   H encourage women suffragists to attack public property.

   J praise the American legal system for protecting private property.

5. What reforms did the Progressives work toward?

   _____
   _____
   _____
   _____
   _____

6. The Geneva Convention of 1864 stated that—

   A the Red Cross would aid all citizens of Switzerland.

   B all men over the age of eighteen must enlist in the military.

   C participants would care for wounded enemy soldiers as well as their own wounded.

   D the use of poisoned gas in warfare was against the law.

88   1 Ⓐ Ⓑ Ⓒ Ⓓ   3 Ⓐ Ⓑ Ⓒ Ⓓ   5 Open-ended
        2 Ⓕ Ⓖ Ⓗ Ⓙ   4 Ⓕ Ⓖ Ⓗ Ⓙ   6 Ⓐ Ⓑ Ⓒ Ⓓ

NAME _____ CLASS _____ DATE _____

7 Fascism is based on the idea that—

- **F** the needs of society are more important than the rights of individuals.
- **G** all human beings are created equal.
- **H** dictatorship is always dangerous and morally wrong.
- **J** a strong monarchy is the best form of government.

8 World War II differed from previous wars because—

- **A** generals of this war employed the strategy of trench warfare.
- **B** it was the first war to target civilians.
- **C** it was the first major war to involve Asia as well as Europe.
- **D** it was the first war in which human rights were violated.

9 The American civil rights movement was most influenced by—

- **F** the example set by leaders of African countries.
- **G** the opposition presented by the Ku Klux Klan.
- **H** the philosophy of "separate but equal" facilities for whites and African Americans.
- **J** Mahandas K. Gandhi's strategy of nonviolent protest.

10 Study the map below. Which of the following countries was not a member of the Warsaw Pact?

- **A** Bulgaria
- **B** Soviet Union
- **C** Poland
- **D** Sweden

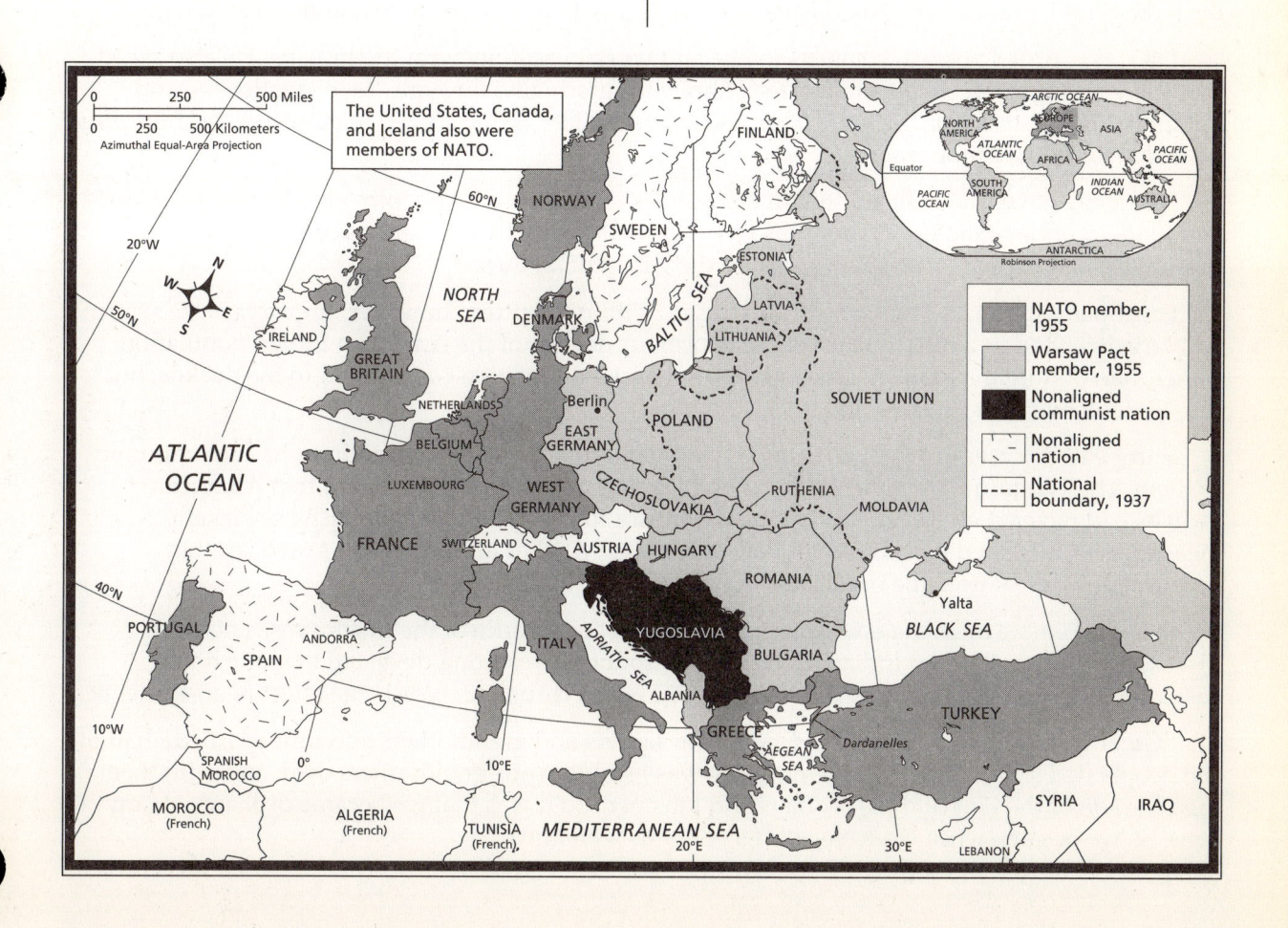

7 Ⓕ Ⓖ Ⓗ Ⓙ   9 Ⓕ Ⓖ Ⓗ Ⓙ
8 Ⓐ Ⓑ Ⓒ Ⓓ   10 Ⓐ Ⓑ Ⓒ Ⓓ

89

Part 2: Practice Tests

Practice Test 1: Reading Comprehension

Sample

When Queen Isabella learned in 1499 that 300 Spanish settlers had returned from the Indies each with an American Indian slave given by Christopher Columbus, she became very angry. In her eyes, American Indians were not slaves. They were supposed to be paid a small allowance for their labor.

Queen Isabella felt that American Indians—

A should all become slaves of the Spanish.

B should be paid for their labors.

C should convert to Roman Catholicism.

D should attend school to learn to read and write.

Directions: For questions 1-37, read each selection carefully. Darken the circle for the correct answer.

Las Casas and Slavery

Some Spaniards protested the harsh treatment of American Indians. One prominent critic, Bartolomé de Las Casas, had lived for some years as an *encomendero* in Cuba. He spent a great deal of time giving the Indians under his care religious instruction. Las Casas, however, began to question the system.

Las Casas urged Spanish colonists to live and work peacefully with the Indians. He also asked that friars and priests convert Indians to Catholicism gradually, through "love, gentleness, and kindness." In his *Apologetic History of the Indies*, published in 1566, he argued that the Indians' humanity equaled that of the Europeans.

"Not only have [the Indians] shown themselves to be very wise peoples and possessed of lively and marked understanding, . . . but they have equaled many diverse nations of the . . . past and present . . . and exceed by no small measure the wisest of all these."

Few Spaniards shared the view of Las Casas. Within a century, however, the *encomienda* system had largely ended as a consequence of the enormous decline of the American Indian population, rather than of humanitarian concerns. Overwork and malnutrition contributed to the decline, but disease took by far the greatest toll.

European diseases proved particularly deadly because the American Indians had no immunity to them. The Western Hemisphere's isolation from the rest of the world meant that American Indians had never been exposed to common illnesses in Europe and Africa such as chickenpox, measles, smallpox, and typhus. When Europeans and Africans arrived in the Americas, they unknowingly introduced the organisms that caused these diseases.

In some remote areas the epidemics preceded the appearance of the Europeans, since the diseases spread easily from Indian to Indian. No doubt the resulting devastation made it much easier for the Spanish to conquer the Indians. One Maya chronicle records the effect of an epidemic.

"Great was the stench of the dead. After our fathers and grandfathers succumbed [died], half of the people fled to the fields . . . The mortality was terrible. Your grandfathers died, and with them died the son of the king and his brothers and kinsmen. So it was that we became orphans, oh, my sons! So we became when we were young. All of us were thus."

1. According to the selection, the majority of Spanish *encomenderos* believed—

   A American Indians were inferior workers, compared with Africans.

   B American Indians would benefit from exposure to European ways.

   C Spanish conquest of inhabited islands was a tragic mistake.

   D American Indians should be treated fairly, as equals of Europeans.

2. The Spanish word <u>encomienda</u> means—

   F outbreak of a deadly disease.

   G conversion to Catholicism.

   H colonial control over the Indians.

   J importation of slave labor from Africa.

3. Las Casas is best described as—

   A a religious fanatic.

   B an abolitionist.

   C an *encomendero*.

   D a humanitarian.

4. Spanish rule of the conquered islands could not be maintained because—

   F so many of the conquered people died.

   G the Spanish Crown would not support the colonies.

   H the Spaniards gradually gave up control of the islands.

   J peoples like the Taino revolted and overthrew the Spaniards.

5. The epidemics among American Indian populations show that—

   A diseases such as chickenpox are usually fatal.

   B the American Indians were biologically weaker than most Europeans.

   C the human body has no immunity to foreign organisms.

   D overwork typically contributes to early death.

6. Paragraph 6 explains that—

   F epidemics among American Indians had taken place even before Europeans arrived.

   G American Indians had been completely free of disease for centuries.

   H the American Indian population had been declining for many years.

   J people living in remote areas are more susceptible to diseases.

7. When one Maya chronicle reported that "the mortality was terrible," he meant—

   A people died after horrible suffering.

   B the death rate was extremely high.

   C many children and elderly people died.

   D the fate of his people was a terrible one.

8. What seems to have been the chief effect of European contact on conquered peoples?

   _____
   _____
   _____
   _____
   _____

An Uneasy Balance: 1845-1861

After bitter debates about slavery, the U.S. House of Representatives passed a "gag resolution" preventing further discussions of petitions against slavery.

The Debate Reopens

The gag rule was a clear sign that tensions had mounted over the issue of slavery. The Missouri Compromise of 1820 had not ended the debate over the spread of slavery. Congress had admitted Arkansas and Michigan to the Union without dispute in 1836 and 1837, respectively. The balance of power in Congress remained the same, however, because Arkansas allowed slavery whereas Michigan did not. Slavery continued to trouble many citizens and politicians. Congressional debates dealing with the subject often ended in violence. Some representatives even carried Bowie knives into the House chamber. The tension erupted in February 1838, when two members of Congress—one from Maine and the other a slaveholder from Kentucky—fought a duel in which the northerner was fatally wounded.

Further trouble arose when the Republic of Texas petitioned for annexation to the United States. The addition of Texas, which permitted slavery, would tip the balance of power in Congress toward the slaveholding states. Northerners responded with resolutions angrily opposing the annexation.

In 1845 Congress settled the issue on terms favorable to the South. Congress not only admitted Texas as a slave state but also added that the state legislature could divide Texas into as many as five states if it wished! At the same time, Congress extended westward the dividing line that had been set by the Missouri Compromise. The Missouri Compromise had banned slavery in the Louisiana Territory north of 36° 30'—Missouri's southern boundary.

The annexation of Texas did not resolve the issue of slavery. The prospect of victory in the Mexican War of 1846 revived the debate. The United States faced the question of whether slavery would be allowed in any territory acquired from Mexico. Pro-slavery and antislavery forces quickly took sides.

To quiet the debate, President James Polk and others suggested extending the Missouri Compromise line westward to the Pacific Ocean. Michigan senator Lewis Cass and Illinois senator Stephen Douglas proposed instead that the territories rely on popular sovereignty. This would allow the citizens of each new territory to vote on whether to permit slavery there.

Neither proposal satisfied the hard-liners. In August 1846, as the House began to consider a bill authorizing funds to buy territory from Mexico after the war, Representative David Wilmot of Pennsylvania introduced an amendment to the bill. His Wilmot Proviso banned slavery in all lands that would be acquired from Mexico. The House generally split along regional lines in its debates on the amendment. Eventually, all but one northern state rallied to its support. Southern states, however, threatened to secede if it became a law. Some southern politicians suggested cutting off all commercial relations with the North. Others proposed refusing to pay debts owed to northern banks and merchants. The Wilmot Proviso was cut from the final bill, much to Wilmot's dissatisfaction. "So dangerous do I believe the spirit and demands of the *Slave Power* . . . if I saw the way open to strike an effectual [effective] and decisive blow against its domination at this time, I would do so."

---

9 The word <u>respectively</u> means—

   F with great respect.

   G mutually.

   H occurring simultaneously.

   J singly, in a particular order.

10 In 1845, how did Congress favor the slaveholding states?

11 The division of Texas into more than one state would have—

A greatly increased the number of slave holding states.

B given the western states a larger territory.

C strengthened the position of northern abolitionists.

D violated the terms of the Missouri Compromise.

12 The term "popular sovereignty" refers to—

F rule by the federal government.

G decision making by the citizens of a territory.

H the annexation of a new territory by the government.

J empowerment of the slaveholding states.

13 The Wilmot Proviso would have—

A extended the area that permitted slavery in the Louisiana Territory.

B prohibited slavery in the Pacific Northwest.

C ended slavery throughout the Union.

D banned slavery in lands acquired from Mexico.

14 Hard-liners disliked the approaches of "popular sovereignty" and the Wilmot Proviso because—

F neither approach would settle completely the issue of slavery.

G both of these approaches favored the position of the slaveholding states.

H both of these approaches favored the position of northerners.

J neither approach respected the wishes of citizens of a territory.

15 In what year did southern states first threaten to secede from the Union?

A 1838

B 1845

C 1846

D 1860

16 What is the main idea of the quotation from Representative David Wilmot, which appears in the last paragraph of the selection?

F Wilmot doubted that the slaveholders would be defeated.

G Wilmot strongly wished to overthrow the slaveholding powers.

H Wilmot had a plan for defeating the slaveholding powers.

J Wilmot believed that war between North and South was inevitable.

17 In this selection, the term "gag rule" refers to—

A the use of physical force against people who wish to speak.

B a law applied to prohibit criminals from defending themselves.

C a means of preventing debate about an issue.

D actions taken to halt violence erupting among political representatives.

18 Between 1845 and 1861, how did the government attempt to deal with the issue of slavery?

_____
_____
_____
_____
_____

The Red Scare

The waves of strikes during 1919 struck fear into the hearts of many Americans. The 1919 strikes were prompted primarily by laborers' desires for a fair deal. Many Americans, however, saw the labor unrest as proof of a coming workers' revolution. Fear that a Bolshevik revolution would erupt in the United States reached its height during the Red Scare. This was a period of anticommunist hysteria during 1919 and 1920.

The Red Scare in the United States was a response to the 1917 revolution in Russia. This revolution resulted in the establishment of a communist government based on Marxist teaching. Under communism, the Russian government owned and controlled all private property, including every industry and factory. In 1919 Russia's Bolshevik leader Vladimir Lenin established an organization called the Communist International. It was designed to encourage a worldwide communist revolution by overthrowing capitalism and free enterprise. The idea that communism might take hold in the United States was frightening to many Americans during 1919.

Karl Marx's message of an unavoidable working-class revolution has been interpreted in many ways over time. It even won some support in the United States. Labor leader Eugene Debs and others formed the Marxist-inspired Socialist Party in 1901. In contrast to the revolutionary Marxism of the Communist Party, Debs's Socialist Party foresaw a peaceful transition to socialism by democratic means. Debs ran for president five times between 1900 and 1920. His Socialist Party platform called for the collective ownership of industry, which was to be achieved by nonviolent means. In the 1912 election Debs received more than 900,000 votes.

When the Bolsheviks seized power in Russia in 1917, most American members of the Socialist Party joined Debs in refusing to support the violent overthrow of the government. A smaller number of American radicals did support the Bolsheviks. These Americans openly embraced Marx's revolutionary ideas. Some believed such a revolution should happen in the United States. Many Americans ignored the differences between socialists and communists. After witnessing the massive strikes of 1919, many people believed that communists, or "Reds," were everywhere. Immigrants, particularly those involved in unions, came under great suspicion. Antiradical fears reached such heights that several elected members of the New York State Assembly were expelled because of their membership in the Socialist Party.

---

19 What important change took place in Russia under the new Communist regime?

   F The Russian government gained control of industry.

   G The workers now owned all factories and businesses.

   H Karl Marx became the leader of the Communist International.

   J Workers organized massive strikes against the government.

20 In contrast to communism, the American economic system is based on—

   A collective ownership of all industry and business.

   B modified socialism.

   C free enterprise and capitalism.

   D government management of private property.

NAME _____ CLASS _____ DATE _____

21. In this selection, the word <u>transition</u> means—
   F passage of time.
   G period of upheaval.
   H type of government.
   J process of change.

22. In what significant way did Eugene Debs's Socialist Party differ from Lenin's Communist Party?

   _____
   _____
   _____
   _____

23. In which year was Debs's Socialist Party most powerful?
   A 1900
   B 1912
   C 1917
   D 1920

24. Most American members of the Socialist Party believed—
   F violence would be necessary in order to overthrow the government.
   G communism and socialism were identical.
   H American government could be changed through peaceful methods.
   J immigrants should not be allowed to join unions.

25. Which group of people did Americans suspect were responsible for the strikes of 1919?
   A working-class men and women
   B Russian political leaders
   C labor organizers
   D communists

26. A Bolshevik was—
   F a communist revolutionary.
   G a Russian worker.
   H an American socialist.
   J a labor leader.

27. The fact that members of the New York State Assembly were expelled because they were socialists shows that—
   A socialism was no longer legal in the United States.
   B most people distrusted elected officials.
   C antiradical fears had come to dominate U.S. politics.
   D communist spies had infiltrated New York state politics.

28. Many Americans were frightened by the labor strikes of 1919 because—
   F they supported big business and capitalism.
   G they were alarmed by the example of the Bolshevik revolution.
   H they did not respect the demands of American workers.
   J the Communist Party was rapidly gaining control of the United States.

Foreign and Domestic Dangers

Amid domestic and political challenges, the Clinton administration confronted a range of global crises. It also wrestled with an increase in terrorism.

As the Cold War faded, regional conflicts intensified. The end of communist rule in Eastern Europe unleashed bitter ethnic and local disputes that had formerly been kept in check by communist authorities. Bosnia and Herzegovina, a region that was once part of Yugoslavia, was torn apart by fighting between Serbs, Croatians, and Slovenes.

The 15 newly independent republics carved out of the former Soviet Union experienced conflict as different groups struggled for power and self-rule. Russia and Ukraine argued over control of the Black Sea fleet, while Christians in the former Soviet republic of Armenia battled with Muslims in neighboring Azerbaijan.

On a brighter note, a new era dawned in South Africa when decades of apartheid came to an end. In 1994 South Africa held its first elections allowing all races to vote. Black civil rights activist Nelson Mandela, who had spent years as a political prisoner in South Africa, won the presidency. Despite conflict between rival political and ethnic groups, South Africa's future looked hopeful.

Elsewhere in Africa, however, turmoil reigned, worsened by famine and grinding poverty. Civil war raged in Liberia, Mali, Somalia, and Zambia. In December 1992, UN forces, including many Americans, launched Operation Restore Hope to provide relief for famine-stricken Somalia. Fighting among rival clans in that country had previously prevented relief workers from getting food and other supplies to starving Somalis. By 1995, when the last UN forces left, the country still had no central government, and Somalia's suffering continued.

Instability also threatened many nations in the Middle East. Islamic fundamentalists battled for political power. Hopes for peace between Palestinians and Israelis were renewed in September 1993, when Palestinian leader Yasir Arafat and Israeli prime minister Rabin signed a peace accord. President Clinton oversaw the signing of the agreement at the White House. He described it as a "historic and honorable compromise."

The peace process suffered a setback in 1995, when a young Israeli with extreme nationalist views assassinated Rabin. In 1996 Benjamin Netanyahu was elected prime minister of Israel and pledged to be less willing to compromise in peace negotiations. U.S. Secretary of State Warren Christopher worked hard to bring the two sides together. Yet new outbreaks of violence between Israeli soldiers and Palestinians in September 1996 made clear that a more peaceful future was far from certain in this troubled region.

---

29 Fighting in Eastern Europe broke out because—

   A the economy in the region was extremely weak.

   B there was a population explosion in these countries.

   C Eastern Europeans were rebelling against communism.

   D communist authorities no longer controlled these regions.

30 What was the major cause of war in Bosnia?

   F Bosnian Muslims sought control of the government.

   G Bosnian Serbs wanted to drive Muslims from the region.

   H The Slovenes attacked Bosnian Serbs.

   J Communists tried to regain control of these nations.

NAME _____ CLASS _____ DATE _____

31. Azerbaijan became the site of—
   A fighting between Armenian Christians and neighboring Muslims.
   B a new, stronger communist government.
   C free elections held in 1994.
   D an Israeli-Arab peace accord.

32. The end of apartheid in South Africa meant that—
   F Nelson Mandela could force whites to leave the country.
   G there was an end to racial tensions in the nation.
   H there would no longer be a president to head the government.
   J all races could now vote in elections.

33. What was the goal of Operation Restore Hope?
   A to bring food and supplies to Somalis
   B to put an end to civil war in African countries
   C to establish a democratic government in South Africa
   D to free Nelson Mandela from prison

34. What occasion caused President Clinton to speak of a "historic and honorable compromise"?
   F the end of apartheid in South Africa
   G the success of UN forces in Somalia
   H the signing of a peace accord between Israelis and Palestinians
   J the end of fighting between Muslims and Serbs

35. By whom was prime minister Rabin assassinated?
   A by a Palestinian who swore vengeance against Israel
   B by a member of his own cabinet
   C by a foreign agent attempting to renew unrest in the area
   D by an Israeli protesting Rabin's moderate stance toward Palestine

36. Rabin's successor, Benjamin Netanyahu, differed from Rabin because—
   F he openly sympathized with Palestinian leaders.
   G he was an Arab, rather than an Israeli.
   H he refused to accept political compromises so readily.
   J he did not acknowledge the support of the United States for Israel.

37. As the 1990s drew to a close, the situation in the Middle East was—
   A uneasy and marked by periods of violence.
   B marked by constant violence and bloody civil wars.
   C completely resolved by political compromises.
   D fairly peaceful and stable.

Practice Test 2: Reading Vocabulary

Sample

Anne Hutchinson was another Puritan who found <u>refuge</u> in Rhode Island after refusing to follow the New England Way.

The word <u>refuge</u> means—

A   insult.

B   distress.

C   sanctuary.

D   exposure.

---

1   A Native American legend tells how the Sky Holder wanted to create people who <u>surpassed</u> all others in beauty, strength, and bravery. <u>Surpass</u> means—

   A   satisfy.

   B   instruct.

   C   exceed.

   D   precede.

2   The word <u>indebted</u> means—

   F   obligated.

   G   generous.

   H   bankrupt.

   J   imprisoned for debt.

3   In 1776, Congress debated Richard Henry Lee's <u>resolution</u> for American independence.

In which sentence does <u>resolution</u> have the same meaning as it does in the sentence above?

   A   The President's air of <u>resolution</u> swayed Congress to his point of view.

   B   The Drama Club passed a <u>resolution</u> to accept three new members each year.

   C   The <u>resolution</u> of the patient's fever is a very good sign.

   D   Tomorrow's newspaper will contain the <u>resolution</u> of today's crossword puzzle.

4   The scholarly nun Sor Juana once explained that she chose to "<u>astutely</u> stock [her] mind with things of beauty." <u>Astutely</u> means—

   F   eagerly.

   G   maturely.

   H   secretly.

   J   wisely.

5   In the 1700s, many French people considered their monarchs <u>frivolous</u> and unconcerned with affairs of state. <u>Frivolous</u> means—

   A   haughty, proud.

   B   selfish, petty.

   C   silly, trivial.

   D   insincere, dishonest.

6   The word <u>ironically</u> means—

   F   without a serious purpose, foolishly.

   G   using words to convey their opposite meaning.

   H   expressing great sympathy and understanding.

   J   hypocritically or untruthfully.

7   > During the Second Great Awakening, membership soared in various Protestant <u>denominations</u>.

   In which sentence does <u>denominations</u> have the same meaning as it does in the sentence above?

   A   The bank teller will ask you what <u>denominations</u> you prefer.

   B   In some secret societies, members have special <u>denominations</u>.

   C   All <u>denominations</u> are welcome in our town's church.

   D   The zoo curator can tell us the <u>denominations</u> of these animals.

8   <u>Dictatorial</u> means the same as—

   F   domineering.

   G   cruel.

   H   well-spoken.

   J   professional.

9   Lewis Cass favored popular sovereignty and publicly <u>denounced</u> the Wilmot Proviso. <u>Denounced</u> means—

   A   promoted.

   B   condemned.

   C   acknowledged.

   D   ridiculed.

10   What is the meaning of the word <u>incompatible</u>?

   _____
   _____
   _____
   _____
   _____

Practice Test 3: Language

Sample

Riley wants to write a biographical sketch of Alexander Hamilton. He has begun his research by using his history textbook and an encyclopedia entry. Now Riley should—

A   begin his first draft of the biographical sketch.

B   read a more detailed study of Alexander Hamilton's life

C   make an outline for his biographical sketch.

D   read at least three full-length biographies of Alexander Hamilton.

Directions: For questions 1-4, darken the circle for the correct answer, or write your answer in the space provided.

> Marisol was assigned to write a report on some aspect of life in America in the 1800s. She chose to research the lives of people living in urban areas.

1   What should Marisol do before she writes her report?

_____
_____
_____
_____

2   Marisol wants to organize her information for the report. Which of the following ideas should be grouped together with information about the urban poor?

A   The merchant and manufacturing class made up a small elite.

B   Mill owners hired many young women from farm families.

C   Technological advances changed the lives of many people.

D   In the 1800s, many epidemics began in overcrowded tenements.

3   Which supporting detail should Marisol include in a paragraph about the rise of an urban middle-class in the 1800s?

F   In middle-class America, work and family life became separate.

G   The population of urban areas rose dramatically between 1800 and 1860.

H   American society always had both rich and poor citizens.

J   Very few women entered the professions in America in the 1800s.

4   To find the most detailed information on her subject, Marisol could use—

A   a series of cross-referenced encyclopedia entries.

B   an atlas showing maps of cities across the nation.

C   a book about the class structure in American society.

D   an almanac from the 1800s.

100

Here is a rough draft of the first part of Marisol's report. Read the rough draft carefully. Then answer questions 5-13.

Urban Life in America in the 1800s

In cities in the 1800s, three distinct groups or social classes developed in America.
(1)
These are the similar ones we have today. The wealthy, the middle-class, and
(2) (3)
the poor. Although there had always been people at both the bottom and the top
(4)
of the social structure, the Market Revolution greatly polarized these groups. In
(5)
addition, a new group emerged it was the American middle-class. Farming families,
(6)
of course, could be either rich or poor depending upon their degree of success.

While life for poor people has always been one of hardship, the existence of
(7)
the urban poor was particularly harsh. Due to the overcrowding and poor ventilation
(8)
of their dwellings, these people often became severely ill. The mortality rate was
(9)
high, and the numbers of babies and children who died during the epidemics was

tragically noted. Diptheria, cholera, and tuberculosis were found common in these
(10)
substandard living conditions.

5   What is the topic sentence of paragraph 1?
    F   1
    G   4
    H   5
    J   6

6   What is the best way to combine sentences 2 and 3?
    _____
    _____
    _____
    _____

7   Which group of words is not a whole sentence?
    A   1
    B   2
    C   3
    D   5

8   Which sentence is a run-on sentence?
    F   1
    G   3
    H   4
    J   5

9   Which sentence does not belong in paragraph 1?
    A   2
    B   3
    C   5
    D   6

10 Which sentence best provides a proper transition between paragraphs 1 and 2?
    F   Throughout the country, recent immigrants tended to belong to the lower social classes.
    G   The bottom of the social structure tells us a great deal about the problems Americans faced.
    H   No social group was immune to health problems.
    J   The rich could afford medicine and doctors, but the poor often could not.

11 What is the best way to rewrite sentence 9?
    _____
    _____
    _____
    _____
    _____

12 In sentence 10, <u>were found common</u> is best written—
    A   were found commonly.
    B   were founded commonly.
    C   were commonly found.
    D   As it is written.

13 Write a sentence that concludes paragraph 2.
    _____
    _____
    _____
    _____

102

Now read the next part of Marisol's rough draft and answer questions 14-22.

In comparison with the urban poor, the middle-class city dwellers dwelled in (11) comfort. They could afford the things that made a home pleasant and sanitary. (12) Bathing facilities and cookware and proper lighting all contributed to the (13) contentment of the typical middle-class family. The middle-class, composing of (14) shopkeepers, artisans, farmers, and some members of the professions, may not have lived in the lap of luxury. But they didn't live in slums, either. (15)

With the emergence of the middle-class, more emphasis was placed on educating (16) the young. Children of the middle-class did not need to leave their homes and (17) became breadwinners. Boys, of course, were more likely to attend school—that is (18) always the way! Young people were expected to learn specialized trades and (19) function as literate members of society. Perhaps because the responsibility for (20) teaching children was lifted from their shoulders, middle-class women became more involved with public matters. Although they did not enter the workforce (21) generally they did make themselves heard as a group on matters of civic interest in many cases.

14 In sentence 11, rewrite the phrase <u>middle-class city dwellers dwelled</u> to avoid repetitious sentence structure.

_____

_____

_____

_____

15 How could sentences 12 and 13 best be combined without losing the meaning of either of the original sentences?

_____

_____

_____

_____

16 In sentence 14, <u>composing of</u> is best written—

   F   composing by.

   G   composes of.

   H   composed of.

   J   As it is written.

17 Which sentence needlessly repeats information provided earlier in the paragraph?

   A   12

   B   13

   C   14

   D   15

18 In sentence 17, <u>and became breadwinners</u> is best written—

   F   and become breadwinners.

   G   and becoming breadwinners.

   H   and have become breadwinners.

   J   As it is written.

19 Which sentence in Marisol's report disrupts the tone of the rest of paragraph?

   A   16

   B   17

   C   18

   D   19

20 What is the best way to rewrite sentence 21 to make it concise?

_____

_____

_____

_____

21 Where should the 2nd paragraph on this page end?

   F   after sentence 18

   G   after sentence 19

   H   after sentence 20

   J   Where it ends now.

22 Write a title for Marisol's report.

_____

_____

_____

_____

NAME _____ CLASS _____ DATE _____

Directions: For questions 23-31, read each sentence carefully. If one of the words is misspelled, darken the circle for that word. If all the words are spelled correctly, then darken the circle for **No mistake.**

23 In the 1400s, <u>Europeans</u> <u>realized</u> that huge <u>profets</u> could be made from
              A   B   C

   trade with Asia. <u>No mistake</u>.
                            D

24 Some <u>crews</u> feared the great <u>expance</u> of ocean to be <u>navigated</u>. <u>No mistake</u>.
              F   G   H   J

25 <u>Ambitous</u> <u>explorers</u> did not <u>tolerate</u> cowardice, however. <u>No mistake</u>.
       A   B   C   D

26 Ferdinand <u>Magellan</u> was <u>acknowledged</u> to be a <u>fearce</u> captain who put down
                     F   G   H

   arguments quickly. <u>No mistake</u>.
                                  J

27 Vasco da Gama <u>eventually</u> <u>completed</u> a sea <u>route</u> to the East. <u>No mistake</u>.
                            A   B   C   D

28 The <u>Portuguese</u> <u>estableshed</u> trading forts <u>throughout</u> Africa and Asia. <u>No mistake</u>.
                F   G   H   J

29 Other <u>European</u> <u>countries</u> grew <u>envius</u> of Portugal's success. <u>No mistake</u>.
                 A   B   C   D

30 They <u>sought</u> <u>access</u> to the rich <u>commercial</u> trade with the Far and Near East. <u>No mistake</u>.
                F   G   H   J

31 <u>Ultimately</u>, <u>commerse</u> between East and West <u>benefited</u> many countries. <u>No mistake</u>.
            A   B   C   D

105

NAME _____ CLASS _____ DATE _____

Practice Test 4: Social Science

Sample

According to archaeologists, the first people to enter North America came from—

A South America.

B Europe.

C Africa.

D Asia.

Directions: For questions 1–38, darken the circle for the correct answer, or write your answer in the space provided.

> "We must consider that we shall be as a city upon a hill. The eyes of all people are upon us. So that if we deal falsely with our God in this work we have undertaken, and so cause Him to withdraw His present help from us, we shall be made a story and a byword through the world."

1 These words were spoken by—

   A the Puritan leader, John Winthrop.

   B Benjamin Franklin.

   C Deputy Governor Thomas Dudley of Massachusetts Bay Colony.

   D the Puritan dissenter, Anne Hutchinson.

2 The repeal of the Stamp Act in 1766 was significant because—

   F it showed the British Crown was ready to grant colonists their independence.

   G it meant that imported luxury goods would no longer be taxable.

   H it halted the tax on printed matter circulating in the colonies.

   J it was the last form of taxation the British Crown imposed on the colonists.

3 The Declaration of Independence turned the colonists into traitors to the English Crown because—

   A it proclaimed the people's right to abolish unfair governments.

   B it openly declared war between the colonies and Britain.

   C it contained articles overthrowing rule by the English monarchy.

   D it established that all men were equals.

4 What did the phrase "Republican Motherhood" represent?

   F the division of the nation's government into a two-party system

   G a movement to give women the right to vote

   H the elevation of American women as moral and civic guides

   J the desire of middle-class wives and mothers to work outside the home

5 How did the framers of the Constitution attempt to resolve sectional differences?

   _____
   _____
   _____
   _____
   _____

6 What is the main purpose of the Bill of Rights?

   A to give African American men the right to vote

   B to limit the power of the central government

   C to create a bicameral legislature

   D to guarantee specific rights to U.S. citizens

106

NAME _____ CLASS _____ DATE _____

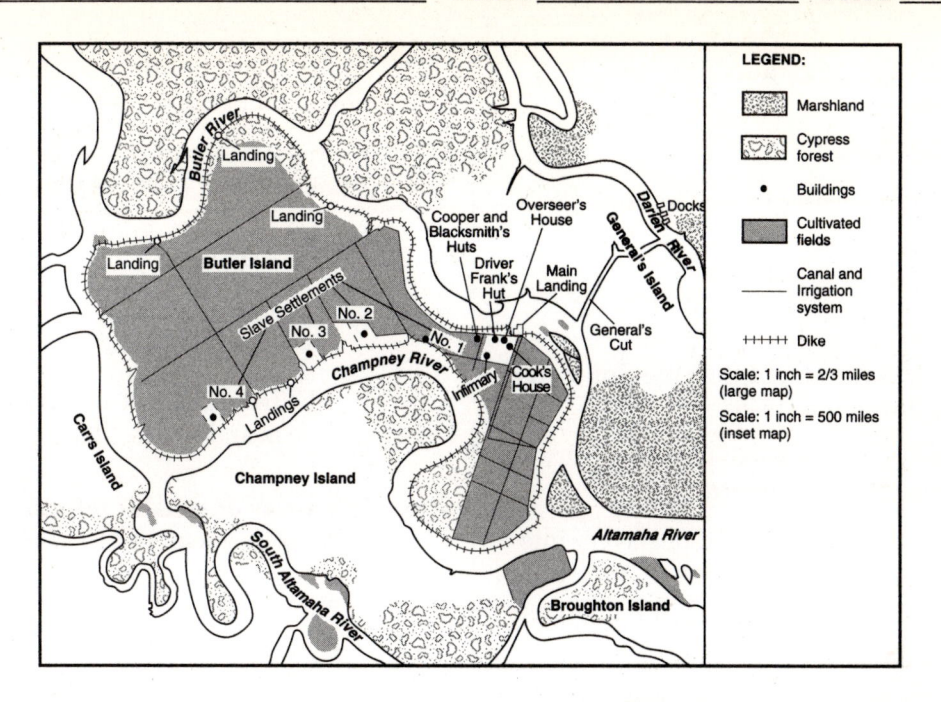

Adapted from map from *Journal of a Residence on a Georgian Plantation in 1838-1893* by Frances Anne Kemble, edited and with an introduction by John A. Scott. Copyright © 1961 by Alfred A. Knopf, Inc. Reprinted by permission of the publisher.

> "The Great Spirit made all things. He gave the white people a home beyond the great waters. He supplied these grounds with game, and gave them to his red children; and he gave them strength and courage to defend them."

7 What can you observe from this map about life on a typical southern plantation?

_____

_____

_____

_____

8 An important result of the Louisiana Purchase was—

F the addition of more slaveholding territories to the nation.

G the opening of the continent's interior to settlement.

H the emigration of many French people into the territory.

J the increase of hostilities between America and Europe.

9 These words are from a speech made by the Shawnee leader Tecumseh to the Osage people. How did Tecumseh want his audience to react?

_____

_____

_____

_____

10 Which was not a reason for the slow growth of industrialization in the south?

A The North was heavily industrialized.

B Southerners tended to invest in money and slaves.

C Southern planters lobbied against taxes that would have fostered manufacturing.

D There was a shortage of factory workers due to the slavery system.

107

NAME _____ CLASS _____ DATE _____

11 **The Shakers and the Mormons are examples of—**
   F the Romantic revival.
   G a movement for social reform.
   H utopian communities.
   J transcendentalist communes.

12 **What was the aim of the Free-Soil Party, which formed in 1848?**
   A to oppose the expansion of slavery into the western territories
   B to support the spread of slavery into the Mexican Cession
   C to advocate the doctrine of popular sovereignty
   D to champion Mexican war-hero Zachary Taylor's candidacy for president

13 **Why was the Supreme Court's decision in the *Dred Scott* case a challenge to the federal government?**
   F It showed that sectional interests affected even Supreme Court decisions.
   G It denied that the federal government had authority to limit slavery.
   H It upheld local laws regarding property rights.
   J It decreed that African Americans were freed.

14 **Why did the South win many of the early battles of the Civil War?**
   A It had a far greater number of troops than the Union Army.
   B Northerners had little passion for the abolitionist cause.
   C President Lincoln did not commit the North's full military powers to these battles.
   D It had a good defensive strategy and superior military leadership.

15 **In the 1800s, political machines were powerful because—**
   F most Americans voted in national elections.
   G Americans did not realize that government was largely corrupt.
   H local officials obtained jobs and services for voters.
   J the federal government had become weak and ineffectual.

16 **What was one major reform the Progressives worked to achieve?**
   _____
   _____
   _____
   _____
   _____

17 **Why did conservative Republicans distrust Theodore Roosevelt?**
   A Roosevelt wanted to reform government and regulate big business.
   B Roosevelt had little background in government.
   C Roosevelt insisted on renaming the Executive Mansion.
   D Roosevelt believed in a "hands off" approach to government.

18 **The term "imperialism" refers to—**
   F the power of the monarchy.
   G rule by a military force.
   H a strong federal government.
   J the quest for colonial empires.

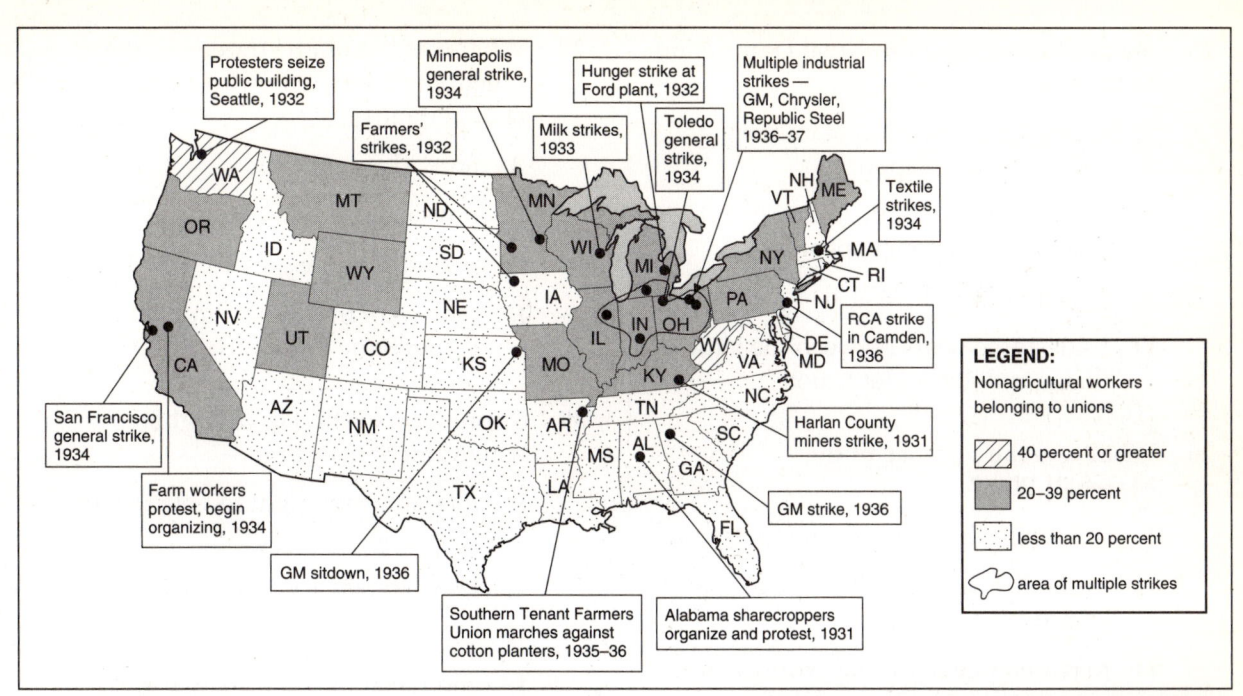

[Map of the United States showing labor strikes and union membership percentages during the Great Depression, with labels including:
- Protesters seize public building, Seattle, 1932
- Minneapolis general strike, 1934
- Hunger strike at Ford plant, 1932
- Multiple industrial strikes—GM, Chrysler, Republic Steel 1936–37
- Farmers' strikes, 1932
- Milk strikes, 1933
- Toledo general strike, 1934
- Textile strikes, 1934
- RCA strike in Camden, 1936
- San Francisco general strike, 1934
- Farm workers protest, begin organizing, 1934
- GM sitdown, 1936
- Southern Tenant Farmers Union marches against cotton planters, 1935–36
- Alabama sharecroppers organize and protest, 1931
- Harlan County miners strike, 1931
- GM strike, 1936

LEGEND: Nonagricultural workers belonging to unions
- 40 percent or greater
- 20–39 percent
- less than 20 percent
- area of multiple strikes]

19 In what region of the world did World War I begin?

  A Great Britain

  B the Balkans

  C Germany

  D Russia

20 The Palmer Raids of 1919 and 1920 were directed against—

  F corrupt local politicians.

  G members of the Ku Klux Klan.

  H suspected radicals.

  J poor tenement dwellers.

21 In the 1920s, a boom in American consumerism occurred largely as a result of—

  A increased trade with European countries.

  B the availability of electrical power.

  C the development of assembly-line manufacturing.

  D the introduction of radio commercials to advertise products.

22 According to the map, during the Great Depression multiple labor strikes took place in—

  F Michigan, Indiana, and Ohio.

  G Kentucky and West Virginia.

  H Washington State.

  J New Jersey and New York.

23 What was an important feature of Franklin D. Roosevelt's administration?

  A a freeze on hiring workers in all federally-controlled jobs

  B a conservative approach to federal spending on social programs

  C large-scale programs which directly helped needy people

  D an emphasis on antitrust laws

24 In the 1920s and 1930s, the United States followed a policy of—

  F détente with most foreign countries.

  G peacekeeping throughout the world.

  H direct intervention in foreign conflicts and civil wars.

  J partial isolationism in dealing with foreign countries.

25 What finally ended the Great Depression in the United States?

- A increased production of military vehicles and weaponry
- B a period of economic inflation and increased consumer spending
- C the end of World War II
- D trade agreements between the United States and the Soviet Union

26 What was the purpose of the Marshall Plan?

- F to rebuild the economy of Japan
- G to stabilize and rebuild Europe after World War II
- H to reintegrate returning World War II veterans into American society
- J to find a permanent place for American women in manufacturing

27 After World War II ended, which group of Americans was most likely to find employment?

- A African American men
- B Hispanic men and women
- C women between the ages of 21 and 45
- D returning war veterans

28 Why did President Eisenhower retire from office in 1961?

- F He had become unpopular with the American public.
- G The constitution limited a president's tenure to two terms.
- H He had reached the age of mandatory retirement.
- J He blamed himself for Cold War tensions between the United States and the U.S.S.R.

29 What was the main strategy of the Freedom Riders who worked for racial equality?

- A nonviolent protest
- B physical combat with white racists
- C petitions to the government
- D redress of illegal discrimination through the law courts

30 Supporters of the Equal Rights Amendment sought to—

- F guarantee the right to vote to women throughout the world.
- G give women access to abortion.
- H bar discrimination on the basis of sex.
- J end racial inequalities in the United States.

31 The United States sent military aid to southern Vietnam in order to—

- A oppose the threat of communism in Southeast Asia.
- B support the Vietnamese leader Ho Chi Minh.
- C support the French government in that country.
- D make the region a colony of the United States.

32 What happened to create the scandal known as "Watergate"?

- F Nixon resigned because of his unsuccessful Vietnam policies.
- G The White House authorized an illegal break-in to spy on the activities of the Democratic National Committee.
- H Vice President Spiro Agnew was convicted of income tax evasion.
- J President Richard Nixon was impeached.

33 The Iran-Contra affair involved—

A a secret sale of missiles to Iran authorized by the U.S. administration.

B terrorism in the war between Israel and the Arab nations.

C a war between Iraq and Iran.

D U.S. support of terrorist groups operating out of Lebanon.

34 During the 1990s, American economists were surprised because—

F the national jobless rate unexpectedly soared.

G the value of the U.S. dollar decreased.

H unemployment, the rate of inflation, and interest rates remained low.

J a period of stagflation began and continued throughout the decade.

35 How did Russian and U.S. expansion differ?

A Only Russia acquired its land through agricultural settlement and conquest.

B Only the United States introduced its own economic and political systems to its holdings.

C In the United States, railways linked vast territories, but Russia did not have a developed railway system.

D Russian expansion was blocked by other empires, but U.S. expansion was not.

36 In the 1870s and 1890s, what caused many bankruptcies and layoffs?

F cycles of boom and bust

G a long period of inflation

H too many overseas consumers of American goods

J major changes in federal and state tax laws

37 What is one important way that developments in technology have helped to spread American popular culture around the world?

_____
_____
_____
_____
_____

38 What is the purpose of the organization known as Amnesty International?

A to grant amnesty, or pardon, to persons convicted of criminal acts

B to provide health services to soldiers of every nation

C to investigate and publicize human rights abuses

D to encourage economic reforms in underdeveloped nations

NAME _____ CLASS _____ DATE _____

Practice Test 5: Listening

For questions 1-16, darken the circle for the word(s) that best complete the sentence you hear.

Sample A
- A a volunteer army
- B the draft
- C local elections
- D a food shortage

1
- A with great severity
- B occurring at the very beginning
- C consequently
- D without much consideration

2
- F inspect or consider for military duty
- G enslave or imprison
- H volunteer for military service
- J engage for military service

3
- A an attitude of hostility or aggression
- B participation in a political cause
- C the state of belonging to neither side
- D the inability to bear arms in battle

4
- F attend to the needs of others
- G conduct a religious service
- H have the status of a clergyman
- J offer advice to others

5
- A faithful to the cause of American independence
- B on the side of the British
- C involved in domestic responsibilities
- D opposed to all forms of violence

6
- F a system of government run by monarchs
- G a system of government where nobles pledge their loyalty to a king
- H a system of government run by elected officials
- J a trading monolpy that controlled the Asian trade routes

7
- A measure Earth's circumference
- B sail completely around the world
- C find new waterways on the Earth
- D make accurate maps of the globe

8
- F falsehoods
- G promises
- H negotiations
- J disputes

9
- A embraced
- B adopted
- C exchanged
- D banished

10
- F permit
- G flatter
- H motivate
- J compel

11
- A pact
- B belief
- C treaty
- D behavior

12
- F adequate
- G important
- H inappropriate
- J successful

13
- A a rumor that travels quickly
- B an outbreak of infectious disease
- C a remark that is exaggerated
- D a cure for an illness

14
- F partnership
- G separation
- H secession
- J competition

15
- A a governor
- B a bishop
- C a vassal
- D a missionary

16
- F determined
- G heated
- H pleased
- J relieved

Sample B

    A people at home did little to help the war effort.

    B slaves were permitted to join the Confederate Army.

    C the conflict lasted longer than anyone had forseen.

    D the morale of the soldiers had fallen.

For questions 17-26, listen to the story. Then darken the circle for the word(s) that best answer the question.

17 A special tax laws
      B enlisted men
      C papers giving a person immunity from military duty
      D laws applying only to slaves

18 F plantation owners avoided military service
      G they were poor and hungry
      H slaves were not drafted
      J they did not believe in slavery

19 A slaves and former slaves
      B wealthy southerners
      C plantation owners
      D poor farmers and working people

20 F unfit for rough work
      G able soldiers
      H irresponsible and lazy
      J loyal to their masters

21 A they believed it violated states' rights
      B they believed it was imposed on them by the federal government
      C they believed it would allow the war to continue indefinitely
      D they believed it was unconstitutional

22 F forcing civilians to enlist in the army
      G housing troops in private farmhouses
      H obtaining food from civilians at low cost
      J attempting to solve food shortages

23 A the fault of the federal government
      B acceptable in some cases
      C unfortunate, but necessary
      D unfair and unconstitutional

24 F they knew they could not stop the soldiers from looting
      G their troops had little food and supplies
      H they wanted to punish civilians who refused to enlist
      J they knew the Union army had the same policy

25 A people would have stormed food stores for free food
      B people would have thrown rotten food away
      C government officials would have distributed free food
      D farmers would have protested the policy of impressment

26 F "Why the South Failed"
      G "Critics of the Confederacy"
      H "The Final Year of the Civil War"
      J "North versus South"

Part 3: Answer Key

Listening Passages for Practice Test 5 (pages 112-113)

Directions: For questions 1-16, the teacher will read each sentence and the four answer choices aloud. Students should listen carefully to the questions and darken the circle for the correct answer.

Sample A

Southern discontent intensified in the spring of 1862, when the Confederacy passed the first <u>conscription</u>, or draft, act in American history. <u>Conscription</u> is another word for—

A a volunteer army
B the draft
C local elections
D a food shortage

1 George Washington <u>initially</u> ordered that no black soldiers could serve in the Continental Army. What does the word <u>initially</u> mean?

A with great severity
B occurring at the very beginning
C consequently
D without much consideration

2 In response, the Continental Army began to <u>enlist</u> free African Americans. What does the word <u>enlist</u> mean?

F inspect or consider for military duty
G enslave or imprison
H volunteer for military service
J engage for military service

3 Both the British and the Patriots tried to respect the tribe's <u>neutrality</u>. What does the word <u>neutrality</u> mean?

A an attitude of hostility or aggression
B participation in a political cause
C the state of belonging to neither side
D the inability to bear arms in battle

4 After one bloody South Carolina battle, women nursed injured American soldiers even as "men dared not come to <u>minister</u> to their wants," according to one observer. In this sentence, what does the word <u>minister</u> mean?

F attend to the needs of others
G conduct a religious service
H have the status of a clergyman
J offer advice to others

5 <u>Loyalist</u> women were also involved in the war effort. In this sentence, what does the word <u>loyalist</u> mean?

A faithful to the cause of American independence
B on the side of the British
C involved in domestic responsibilities
D opposed to all forms of violence

6 In 509 B.C. the city-state of Rome established a <u>republic</u>. A <u>republic</u> is—

F a system of government run by monarchs.
G a system of government where nobles pledge their loyalty to a king.
H a system of government run by elected officials.
J a trading monopoly that controlled the Asian trade routes.

7 To <u>circumnavigate</u> the globe means to—

A measure Earth's circumference.
B sail completely around the world.
C find new waterways on Earth.
D make accurate maps of the globe.

114

8 Theyendanegea, an important Mohawk chief known to colonists as Joseph Brant, had received <u>assurances</u> from the British that they would protect the Iroquois land rights. <u>Assurances</u> mean—

F falsehoods.
G promises.
H negotiations.
J disputes.

9 During the American Revolution, women loyal to the British cause were also involved in the war effort. Although many fled their homes or were <u>exiled</u>, others spied for the British army and aided British prisoners. Another word for <u>exiled</u> is—

A embraced.
B adopted.
C exchanged.
D banished.

10 In 1774 the British Parliament responded to the Boston Tea Party by passing the <u>Coercive</u> Arts. To <u>coerce</u> means to—

F permit.
G flatter.
H motivate.
J compel.

11 In 1785 James Madison declared, "Religion . . . must be left to the <u>conviction</u> and conscience of every man." The word <u>conviction</u> means —

A pact.
B belief.
C treaty.
D behavior.

12 Most poor southern whites lived on lands <u>unsuitable</u> for producing cash crops. When something is <u>unsuitable</u>, it is—

F adequate.
G important.
H inappropriate.
J successful.

13 He pretended to have the power to spread the smallpox <u>plague</u>. The word <u>plague</u> means—

A a rumor that travels quickly.
B an outbreak of infectious disease.
C a remark that is exaggerated.
D a cure for an illness.

14 Many American Indian groups formed <u>alliances</u> to prevent the loss of their lands but were unable to stop the flood of settlers to the region. <u>Alliance</u> means—

F partnership.
G separation.
H secession.
J competition.

15 To reward Christopher Columbus for his discoveries, Ferdinand and Isabella agreed that the mariner would be knighted, appointed an admiral, and made <u>viceroy</u>. The word <u>viceroy</u> means—

A a governor.
B a bishop.
C a vassal.
D a missionary.

16 The slaveholders' anger was slightly <u>appeased</u> by the capture of Nat Turner. <u>Appeased</u> means—

F determined.
G heated.
H pleased.
J relieved.

Directions: For questions 17-26, the teacher will read the passage and the questions pertaining to the passage aloud. Students should listen carefully to the passage and questions and take notes on a separate sheet of paper. Then, students should darken the circle for the correct answer.

Sample B

Although many people on the homefront worked to keep the war effort going and morale high, others voiced their displeasure with the war. Opposition grew as the bloody conflict dragged on longer than anyone had envisioned.

Opposition to the war grew because—

A people at home did little to help the war effort.

B slaves were permitted to join the Confederate army.

C the conflict lasted longer than anyone had foreseen.

D the morale of the soldiers had fallen.

Southern Opposition to the Civil War

The southern draft placed the major burden for fighting on poor farmers and working people. Draft exemptions for large plantation owners—who had led the Confederacy into war—created tension between wealthy southerners and nonslaveholding whites. Many white southerners openly criticized the policy, claiming that it proved the conflict was a "rich man's war and a poor man's fight," as Confederate private Sam Watkins wrote in his memoirs. In response, plantation owners argued that some slaveholders had to remain at home to keep their slaves from running off. The Confederacy needed food and cloth, and few southerners believed that slaves would work without constant supervision.

Other southerners opposed the draft because they believed it violated states' rights and freedom. These were the very principles that had led southern states to secede from the Union in the first place. Georgia governor Joseph E. Brown argued that "no act of the Government of the United States prior to the secession struck a blow at constitutional liberty so [fatal] as has been stricken by this conscription act."

As the war intensified, the Confederacy began to allow soldiers to pay farmers prices far below the market value for food, animals, and other property. Called robbery by many farmers, this policy of impressment placed a heavy burden on food-producing families and led to serious food shortages. Fear of starvation led to food riots in Alabama, Georgia, and North Carolina.

17 **What were draft exemptions?**

A special tax laws

B enlisted men

C papers giving a person immunity from military duty

D laws applying only to slaves

18 **Many white southerners were angry because—**

F plantation owners avoided military service.

G they were poor and hungry.

H slaves were not drafted.

J they did not believe in slavery.

19 **The greater part of the Confederate army was made up of—**

A slaves and former slaves.

B wealthy southerners.

C plantation owners.

D poor farmers and working people.

20 **It is clear that many white southerners regarded slaves as—**

F unfit for rough work.

G able soldiers.

H irresponsible and lazy.

J loyal to their masters.

21 **Why did many southerners oppose the draft?**

A They believed it violated states' rights.

B They believed it was imposed on them by the federal government.

C They believed it would allow the war to continue indefinitely.

D They believed it was unconstitutional.

22 The policy of impressment involved—

    F forcing civilians to enlist in the army.

    G housing troops in private farmhouses.

    H obtaining food from civilians at low cost.

    J attempting to solve food shortages.

23 Georgia governor Joseph E. Brown felt that conscription was—

    A the fault of the federal government.

    B acceptable in some cases.

    C unfortunate, but necessary.

    D unfair and unconstitutional.

24 Why did the Confederacy allow the policy of impressment to continue?

    F They knew they could not stop the soldiers from looting.

    G Their troops had little food and supplies.

    H They wanted to punish civilians who refused to enlist.

    J They knew the Union army had the same policy.

25 What would have taken place at a food riot?

    A people would have stormed food stores for free food

    B people would have thrown rotten food away

    C government officials would have distributed free food

    D farmers would have protested the policy of impressment

26 What would be a good title for this passage?

    F "Why the South Failed"

    G "Critics of the Confederacy"

    H "The Final Year of the Civil War"

    J "North versus South"

ANSWERS

**Activity 1 Reading Comprehension:
Prehistory**

1. B climate changes throughout the Americas
2. J objects crafted by humans
3. A why different languages and cultures developed
4. G The identification of animals was very important to Native American peoples.
5. C Native Americans did not keep written records.
6. Answers will vary, but student's response could include:
   - myths and legends are sources of history and traditions
7. G The climate grew warmer and drier.
8. Answers will vary, but student's response could include:
   - variations existed because of differences in environments
   - different types of animals lived in different places and required specific hunting methods

**Activity 2 Reading Vocabulary:
Empires of the Americas**

1. C governor
2. J Further study is needed of our complex ecosystems.
3. A conquered
4. H traditions
5. A resistance
6. Answers will vary, but student's response could include:
   - a condition of the body caused by eating too little food
   - a condition of the body caused by eating the wrong foods
7. G died
8. C honored
9. F consider
10. Answers will vary, but student's response could include:
    - abnormally lean or thin

**Activity 3 Language:
Life in Colonial Massachusetts**

1. C Hoped to find fertile land and a temperate climate.
2. J The Puritans brought their high moral and ethical principles to the colony they founded in Massachusetts.
3. C 6
4. Answers will vary, but student's response could include:
   - in the Puritan community, cooperation between church and state was essential

Activity 4 Social Science: Independence!

1. C American Indian uprisings
2. G tax printed matter circulating in the American colonies
3. A they feared the East India Company would monopolize the tea trade
4. Answers will vary, but student's response could include:
   - bitterly cold weather
   - lack of clothing to protect soldiers from the elements
   - disease and illness plagued the camps caused by poorly prepared food, contaminated water supplies, and unsanitary conditions
   - constant troop shortages
5. F the Muddy River and the Charles River
6. C The colonists feared these officials would be free to ignore colonial demands.
7. J Britain's attempts to impose certain taxes on the colonists

**Activity 5 Reading Comprehension:
From Confederation to Federal Union**

1. B to persuade him to support laws giving legal rights to women
2. F reasonable men do not dominate or mistreat women
3. C without fear of punishment
4. Answers will vary, but student's response could include:
   - she wanted to remind him that ensuring equality and independence for the American colonies extended to women, too
5. J the colonists' efforts to achieve independence from Britain

118

6	C	the growing desire of women for legal and social equality
7	F	Men know that they do not actually dominate or control women.
8	D	he believes loyalists to be politically weak and misguided

Activity 6 Reading Vocabulary: A Strong Start for the Nation

1. **B** unwilling
2. Answers will vary, but student's response could include:
   - confirmation
   - approval
   - endorsement
3. **J** George Washington's leadership was considered critical to the success of the Patriots.
4. **A** soundness
5. **G** increase
6. **D** an act that is used as an example
7. **F** inappropriate
8. **B** eventually or finally
9. **H** A speech and a luncheon constituted the proceedings of our club.
10. Answers will vary, but student's response could include:
    - kidnapping
    - forcing someone to do something
    - seizing something for public use
11. **C** important

Activity 7 Language: Nationalism and Economic Growth

1. **A** 1
2. **J** 4
3. **A** 5
4. **G** 6
5. **C** reveals
6. **F** Hawthorne, if he is the narrator,
7. Answers will vary, but student's response could include:
   - the narrator does not know, but he looks on with great curiosity
8. **D** His detached viewpoint marks the narrator as a natural writer.
9. Answers will vary, but student's response could include:
   - "The Narrator's Influence in Nathaniel Hawthorne's *Sights from a Steeple*"

Activity 8 Social Science: Regional Societies

1. **D** The South had the slowest growth in urban population.
2. **G** the factory system
3. **A** the reduction of the workday to ten hours
4. **H** Irish Catholics
5. **B** a nativist group with strong anti-Catholic feelings
6. **F** Eli Whitney's invention of the cotton gin
7. **C** by small-scale farming
8. **G** practiced in urban centers as well as rural areas
9. **D** the assignment of slaves into specialized jobs
10. Answers will vary, but student's response could include:
    North
    - industry and manufacturing oriented
    - labor unions
    South
    - agriculturally oriented with slave labor

Activity 9 Reading Comprehension: Women and Reform

1. **C** the expectation that women would focus all their activities on household matters
2. **J** middle-class women
3. **A** able to read and write
4. **H** 1840s
5. **B** the establishment of tax-supported elementary schools
6. **J** An educated populace would be democratic and productive.
7. Answers will vary, but student's response could include:
   - a literate and disciplined workforce
   - equal quality of education
8. **B** inadequate

Activity 10 Reading Vocabulary: Expansion and Conflict

1. B obvious
2. F maneuver
3. D The messenger delivered the letter with dispatch.
4. G prestige
5. A following
6. Answers will vary, but student's response could include:
   - to give up
   - to sacrifice
7. G Missionaries promoted the conversion of some tribes to Christianity.
8. C punish
9. Answers will vary, but student's response could include:
   - disorder
   - confusion
10. J penniless

Activity 11 Language: The Abolitionist Movement

1. A 1
2. G , the abolitionists, said, "No!"
3. Answers will vary, but student's response could include:
   - Abolitionists had existed before the Fugitive Slave Act of 1850 when it became a crime to help runaway slaves, even outside the slave states.
4. B 7
5. H It meant that slavery was expanding into the free territories.
6. Answers will vary, but student's response could include:
   - Well-known orators, such as ex-slave Frederick Douglass, spoke against slavery and urged people to defy the new law.
7. A responded to this call by forming mobs
8. J 13
9. Answers will vary, but student's response could include:
   The Underground Railroad, a loose system of safe houses and conductors who led slaves to freedom, was formed by individuals.

Activity 12 Social Science: The Civil War

1. C opposing the further expansion of slavery
2. F the Confederates bombarded Fort Sumter
3. B slave states that did not secede from the union
4. F More than one-third of southerners were slaves.
5. C Robert E. Lee
6. F the federal government's naval blockade of the South
7. C lack of food and supplies
8. J The Union needed to gain control of the Mississippi River.
9. A He wanted to seize provisions from the enemy.
10. Answers will vary but student's responses could include:
    - President Lincoln was dissatisfied with his other leaders
    - Grant was a good soldier and was relentless in his attacks on the Confederates

Activity 13 Reading Comprehension: Reconstruction and the New South

1. B sympathetic to the former Confederates
2. F belonging to the same period of time
3. C to impose financial penalties on supporters of the Confederacy
4. F he was extremely prejudiced against African Americans
5. D The state did not ratify the Thirteenth Amendment.
6. H with great enthusiasm
7. B He was sympathetic to the feelings of prejudiced white citizens.
8. J He allowed high ranking ex-Confederates to hold political office.
9. B to limit the freedom of African Americans
10. Answers will vary, but student's response could include:
    - his prejudices against African Americans encouraged former Confederates to adopt laws limiting the freedom of former slaves
    - his refusal to sign the Freedman's Bureau Bill

Activity 14   Reading Vocabulary: The Western Crossroads

1. C cruel conduct
2. J broke
3. A overwhelmed
4. G The assimilation of Yan's parents was incomplete; they spoke their original language and did not mingle with their American neighbors.
5. C a large-scale operation
6. F likely to become
7. C The reservation was located in a remote part of the state.
8. J dangerous
9. B bring into being
10. Answers will vary, but student's response could include:
    - to set apart
    - to isolate

Activity 15   Language: The Second Industrial Revolution

1. Answers will vary, but student's response could include:
    - Before the Civil War, the railroad system in the United States was not fully developed.
2. C people who planned to travel
3. J 4
4. B 6
5. H major improvements had been made
6. Answers will vary, but student's response could include:
    - Between 1860 and 1869, major improvements had been made, and by 1869 the country had its first transcontinental railroad.
7. A This was an historic occasion to celebrate, as the railways now truly served the nation's people.
8. G Trunk lines, which were major railroads,
9. C Now passengers could travel conveniently from large cities to small towns.

Activity 16   Social Science: The Transformation of American Society

1. C Protestants from northwestern Europe
2. F escape religious or political persecution
3. Answers will vary, but student's response could include:
    - immigrants were given a physical exam and were questioned about their backgrounds
    - people with diseases, mental disorders, or criminal records were sent back
4. B crowded urban areas
5. J the nativist movement in the United States
6. A doubled
7. H the development of mass transit systems
8. B the relative wages of the working poor
9. J the East Side of Manhattan
10. Answers will vary, but student's response could include:
    - provide educational and cultural opportunities to the poor
    - improve living conditions in the neighborhoods

Activity 17   Reading Comprehension: The Populist Movement

1. C production by farmers that exceeded public consumption
2. Answers will vary, but student's response could include:
    - farmers had borrowed money to pay for their land and buy new equipment, but had put their farms up as security
    - when farmers couldn't repay their loans, they lost their farms
3. J give them a larger market and increased profits
4. B charges for hauling farm produce kept rising
5. J declines
6. A the banks and the railroads
7. G They hoped to force banks and railroads to make reforms.
8. D avoid dealing with distributors and therefore save money
9. F the standardization of railroad freight and grain-storage rates
10. Answers will vary, but student's response could include:
    - farm profits plunged because of oversupply of crops and animals and diminishing demand for products
    - farmers lost their farms because they were unable to repay their loans

Activity 18 Reading Vocabulary: The Age of Reform

1. **B** The mayor was removed from office because he was proved corrupt.
2. Answers will vary, but student's response could include:
   - advancing
   - up-and-coming
   - activist
   - forward-looking
3. **J** lower or secondary
4. **A** indifference
5. **H** unexpectedly early
6. **D** illuminated
7. **H** avoidance of alcoholic beverages
8. **B** immortality
9. **F** Feminists protest economic discrimination against women.
10. Answers will vary, but student's response could include:
    - impart
    - implant
    - mix in

Activity 19 Language: Progressive Politicians

1. **B** 2
2. Answers will vary, but student's response could include:
   - Perhaps his sense of self resulted from being raised by two parents who had very different beliefs and outlooks.
3. **H** 4
4. **A** In 1898 the now-robust Roosevelt became a national hero during the Spanish-American War.
5. **J** 9
6. **A** some of whom distrusted
7. **G** 11
8. **C** he also could accept
9. **J** 16

Activity 20 Social Science: America and the World

1. **B** find new markets and natural resources
2. **H** cultural bias and a superior attitude
3. **A** Pacific trading and whaling ships
4. **J** A group of Chinese nationalists attacked Western missionaries and traders.
5. **D** the United States should not violate the ideals expressed in its own Declaration of Independence
6. **F** he believed newspapers should shape public opinion and policy
7. **B** Russia
8. **G** receives military protection but gives up some of its political rights
9. **A** he felt the Monroe Doctrine excused excessive territorial aggression
10. Answers will vary, but student's response could include:
    - its enforcement of the Monroe Doctrine
    - it joined European powers in trying to colonize uncolonized areas
    - its involvement in Cuba and Philippines

Activity 21 Reading Comprehension: The United States Goes to War

1. **B** attack by German naval forces
2. **F** the torpedoing of the *Lusitania*
3. **D** American leaders believed Europeans should fight their own war
4. **G** supportive of the Allies
5. **A** negotiator
6. Answers will vary, but student's response could include:
   - widespread promotion of ideas
   - ideas used to further one's cause or damage another's
7. **H** the British suspected American ships of carrying goods to the enemy
8. **D** by charging that the ship was carrying arms for Britain
9. **H** He believed President Wilson had violated his neutrality policy.
10. Answers will vary, but student's response could include:
    - the sinking of the *Lusitania*, killing 128 Americans
    - Germany's unrestricted submarine warfare.

Activity 22 Reading Vocabulary: A Turbulent Decade

1. Answers will vary, but student's response should include:
   - to disband troops
   - to move from wartime to peacetime
2. **C** persuaded
3. **F** threaten
4. **C** Some colleges strive to recruit students with athletic ability.
5. **H** sharing the same views
6. **B** dismissed
7. **J** formal questioning

8   Answers will vary, but student's response could include:
   - to encourage
   - to motivate
9   C   Officials at the soccer game had to suppress the riotous behavior of fans.
10 F   guilty

Activity 23   Language: Henry Ford

1   Answers will vary, but student's response could include:
   - One man, Henry Ford, did more to expand the automobile industry than any other person.
2   C   3
3   F   Ford's new method reduced the time it took to assemble a Model T engine by half.
4   C   6
5   J   7
6   A   did not necessarily improve
7   G   9
8   C   discriminatory practices
9   J   13
10 Answers will vary, but student's response could include:
   - "Growth of the Auto Industry"

Activity 24   Social Science: America and the World: Prosperity Shattered

1   D   the faith of Americans in the nation's economic prosperity
2   G   a period of rising stock prices
3   A   a major banking crisis
4   J   huge war debts owed by European countries
5   A   to finance the creation of farmers' cooperatives
6   H   the gap in income between rich and poor
7   D   15 million
8   G   skilled workers without jobs
9   B   West Virginia and Washington State
10 Answers will vary, but student's response could include:
   - money lent to big business would not filter down quickly enough to the ordinary citizen who needed it the most

Activity 25   Reading Comprehension: Life in the New Deal Era

1   C   much of the Great Plains region
2   G   a severe lack of rainfall
3   A   planting trees to create a windbreak
4   J   find work harvesting crops
5   B   dust clouds could travel many hundreds of miles
6   J   competition from other farm workers seeking jobs
7   C   organizing a strong labor union
8   F   lowered pay
9   C   increased job competition meant lower pay for workers
10 Answers will vary, but student's response could include:
   - organized and joined labor unions
   - relocated their homes and families in hopes of finding jobs

Activity 26   Reading Vocabulary: The Road to War

1   B   payments made for damages
2   Answers will vary, but student's response could include:
   - withdrawal from world affairs
3   J   shameful
4   A   Our ultimate goal is to prevent another world war from occurring.
5   G   a reduction in size of a country's military
6   C   to do away with
7   F   power
8   B   The integrity of the Union was Abraham Lincoln's greatest concern.
9   J   penalties
10 Answers will vary, but student's response could include:
   - authorized delay

Activity 27   Language: World War II

1. **A** , a year before the United States joined the Allies to fight the Axis Powers,
2. Answers will vary, but student's response could include:
   - British Prime Minister Winston Churchill probably did not know it, but he made a historical pronouncement when he said, "The Battle of Britain is about to begin . . . The whole fury of the enemy must very soon be turned upon us."
3. **H** 6
4. **D** 8
5. **F** were truly impressed
6. **B** In addition to the home troops, Canadians and Australians fought in the Battle of Britain.
7. **F** 11
8. **C** While soldiers battled the air attacks
9. **G** Later, the Axis Powers began bombing residential areas as well.

Activity 28   Social Science: The Cold War

1. **D** the United Nations
2. **G** bring Nazi war criminals to trial
3. **C** the founding of the state of Israel
4. **J** Japan
5. **A** Zionist David Ben-Gurion
6. **G** the struggle between the United States and the Soviets for political dominance
7. **C** limiting the spread of communism throughout the world
8. **J** the European Recovery Program
9. **A** protect the member nations from foreign attack
10. Answers will vary, but student's response could include:
    - the United States refused to recognize the communist government, the People's Republic of China, and continued to financially support the Nationalists as China's legal government

Activity 29   Reading Comprehension: The Challenges of Peace

1. **C** The return of veterans meant increased competition for jobs.
2. Answers will vary, but student's response could include:
   - created the GI Bill of Rights
   - passed the Employment Act of 1946
   - established the Council of Economic Advisers
3. **F** The GI Bill allowed many more people to attend college to prepare themselves for better careers.
4. **D** manufacturing more consumer goods
5. **J** inflation
6. **D** An economic depression occurred after World War I.
7. **C** government policies encouraged employers to hire veterans.
8. **B** women were no longer encouraged to hold jobs outside the home
9. **G** Foreign countries had not been able to produce enough food.
10. Answers will vary, but student's response could include:
    - gave veterans loans to start businesses and buy homes
    - gave money to attend college
    - provided pensions

Activity 30   Reading Vocabulary: The New Frontier and the Great Society

1. **B** Last year, Congress focused on domestic issues rather than foreign affairs.
2. **F** make use of for selfish purposes
3. **D** one who comes before
4. **H** governments ruled by a few people
5. **A** incapable
6. **G** threaten
7. **D** agreed or cooperated
8. **H** Whether the senator will run for office again is a matter of intense speculation.
9. **A** unavoidable
10. Answers will vary, but student's response could include:
    - a special kind of charm that inspires devotion and allegiance

Activity 31 Language: Martin Luther King Jr. and the Civil Rights Movement

1. D — 4
2. G — who were more radical
3. Answers will vary, but student's response could include:

   But even now, thirty years after his murder, Martin Luther King Jr. is remembered by many as the most powerful figure in the civil rights movement of the 1960s.
4. A — 10
5. H — his protest on behalf of Rosa Parks
6. C — 13
7. J — 14
8. B — after sentence 11

Activity 32 Social Science: Struggles for Change

1. D — were dissatisfied with their roles as homemakers
2. G — women could have legal abortions during the first trimester of pregnancy
3. A — helping migrant agricultural workers obtain fair pay
4. Answers will vary, but student's response could include:
   - Both Chávez and King used Gandhi's example of nonviolent resistance to bring about social change
5. J — It represented Mexican Americans who had land illegally taken from them.
6. C — Mexican Americans throughout the United States
7. F — the right to self-government for American Indians
8. Answers will vary, but student's response could include:
   - passed laws requiring wheelchair ramps and special parking spaces at public facilities
   - many buildings began to include signs in braille
9. D — changes in the values held by people of different ages
10. G — creating art that would appeal to popular tastes

Activity 33 Reading Comprehension: War in Vietnam

1. C — to prevent the communists from controlling southern Vietnam
2. F — believable or reliable
3. D — There were more votes than there were voters.
4. F — He knew he would lose to Ho Chi Minh.
5. C — he was brutal toward people who opposed him politically
6. J — was politically influenced by foreign powers
7. B — Many people wanted to overthrow President Diem.
8. H — southern Vietminh who were against President Diem
9. A — Kennedy authorized more U.S. forces to fight the Vietcong.
10. Answers will vary, but student's response could include:
    - President Kennedy increased the number of U.S. military advisers in South Vietnam
    - U.S. forces were given permission to engage in direct combat
    - Congress passed the Tonkin Gulf Resolution in 1964

Activity 34 Reading Vocabulary: From Nixon to Carter

1. B — intensified
2. F — a suspension of trade
3. C — matter that is discharged into the air
4. J — political authority
5. B — power to act effectively
6. H — The trial was suspended due to a problem with one of the witnesses.
7. A — having the same relationship to one another
8. F — endlessly
9. D — A civil war is always a critical period in a nation's history.
10. Answers will vary, but student's response could include:
    - to come between
    - to settle or influence

125

Activity 35 Language: Women in the Military

1. Answers will vary, but student's response could include:
   - Until recently, women in the military were not allowed to serve as combat pilots.
2. D 6
3. F 7
4. B 8
5. H This creates
6. D 10
7. F Operation Desert Storm, and brought
8. B One high-ranking officer, Air Force colonel Douglas Kennett,
9. Answers will vary, but student's response could include:
   - They helped win the war and that should not be forgotten.

Activity 36 Social Science: Life in the 1990s and Beyond

1. B renewal of the nation
2. J There was a marked increase in the number of women running for political office.
3. B reducing the national debt
4. F Communist authorities no longer kept these tensions under control.
5. Answers will vary, but student's response could include:
   - the policy of racial segregation and political and economic discrimination against people of color
6. C Serbian efforts to drive Muslims out of Bosnia.
7. J cut popular social and environmental programs
8. B a booming stock market
9. F widespread computer failure predicted for the year 2000
10. Answers will vary, but student's response could include:
    - aided in the exportation of American popular culture
    - trade in American consumer products increased

Activity 37 Reading Comprehension: Industrialism and Empire

1. D reasons
2. F the reasons underlying Western imperialism
3. B white westerners felt themselves superior to people of other backgrounds
4. H Western manufacturers needed raw materials found in the East.
5. D he believed that stronger nations could and should rule weaker countries
6. Answers will vary, but student's response could include:
   - steamships extended imperial power on the seas and needed fuel for the ships
7. H saved money on labor when they gained control of foreign countries
8. A possible
9. H Western powers would defeat weaker nations because of superior weaponry.
10. B the Africans did not understand the effectiveness of modern weaponry

Activity 38 Reading Vocabulary: The Rise of the Global Economy

1. A singleness
2. H easy to injure
3. B forced
4. F That country has a disposition to maintain the peace.
5. Answers will vary, but student's response could include:
   - to engage in business to make a profit
6. C motivating
7. J Cotton and rice were staples of the southern economy.
8. B spoils quickly
9. G actually
10. A compensation

Activity 39 Language: The Movement of People and Ideas

1. C Only a few years ago,
2. Answers will vary, but student's response could include:
   - Only a few years ago, I was in the middle of writing a research paper and needed to find more facts to include.
3. F 4
4. D 6
5. J 8
6. Answers will vary, but student's response could include:
   - Yesterday, without any trouble, I once again found myself collecting information for a school assignment.
7. C 11
8. G sites
9. A The speed of the Internet had made my research a snap.

Activity 40 Social Science: The Struggle for Human Rights

1. B It influenced the French to overthrow their monarchy.
2. J release enslaved men and women from captivity
3. A European and Latin American countries were abolishing slavery
4. H encourage women suffragists to attack public property
5. Answers will vary, but student's response could include:
   - problems caused by industrialization and urban growth
   - governmental corruption
   - corporate monopolies
   - the wasting of natural resources
   - limiting child labor
6. C participants would care for wounded enemy soldiers as well as their own wounded
7. F the needs of society are more important than the rights of individuals
8. B it was the first war to target civilians
9. J Mahandas K. Gandhi's strategy of nonviolent protest
10. D Sweden

Part 2

Practice Test 1: Reading Comprehension

Sample B should be paid for their labors

Las Casas and Slavery

1. B American Indians would benefit from exposure to European ways
2. H colonial control over the Indians
3. D a humanitarian
4. F so many of the conquered people died
5. C the human body has no immunity to foreign organisms
6. F epidemics among American Indians had taken place even before Europeans arrived
7. B the death rate was extremely high
8. Answers will vary, but student's response could include:
   - introduction of epidemics that led to a high mortality rate

An Uneasy Balance: 1845-1861

9. J singly, in a particular order
10. Answers will vary, but student's response could include:
    - admitted Texas as a slave state with the ability to further split the existing state into five separate states
11. A greatly increased the number of slave-holding states
12. G decision making by the citizens of a territory
13. D banned slavery in lands acquired from Mexico
14. F neither approach would settle completely the issue of slavery
15. C 1846
16. G Wilmot strongly wished to overthrow the slaveholding powers.
17. C a means of preventing debate about an issue
18. Answers will vary, but student's response could include:
    - continually extended the Missouri Compromise line westward until ultimately it reached the Pacific Ocean

127

The Red Scare

19	F	The Russian government gained control of industry.
20	C	free enterprise and capitalism
21	J	process of change
22		Answers will vary, but student's response could include:

- Debs advocated peaceful, nonviolent means of protest versus Lenin's policy of violence
- Debs advocated collective ownership of industry versus Lenin's government ownership of all private property

23	B	1912
24	H	American government could be changed through peaceful methods
25	D	communists
26	F	a communist revolutionary
27	C	antiradical fears had come to dominate U.S. politics
28	G	they were alarmed by the example of the Bolshevik Revolution

Foreign and Domestic Dangers

29	D	communist authorities no longer controlled these regions
30	G	Bosnian Serbs wanted to drive Muslims from the region.
31	A	fighting between Armenian Christians and neighboring Muslims
32	J	all races could now vote in elections
33	A	to bring food and supplies to Somalis
34	H	the signing of a peace accord between Israelis and Palestinians
35	D	by an Israeli protesting Rabin's moderate stance toward Palestine
36	H	he refused to accept political compromises so readily
37	A	uneasy and marked by periods of violence

Practice Test 2: Reading Vocabulary

Sample	C	sanctuary
1	C	exceed
2	F	obligated
3	B	The Drama Club passed a resolution to accept three new members each year.
4	J	wisely
5	C	silly, trivial
6	G	using words to convey their opposite meaning
7	C	All denominations are welcome in our town's church.
8	F	domineering
9	B	condemned
10		Answers will vary, but student's response could include:

- mismatched
- contrary
- clashing

Practice Test 3: Language

Sample	B	read a more detailed study of Alexander Hamilton's life
1		Answers will vary, but student's response could include:

- begin to gather research information from textbook, encyclopedia entries, Internet searches

2	D	In the 1800s, many epidemics began in overcrowded tenements.
3	F	In middle-class America, work and family life became separate.
4	C	a book about the class structure in American society
5	F	1
6		Answers will vary, but student's response could include:

- These social classes—the wealthy, the middle class, and the poor—still exist today.

7	C	3
8	J	5
9	D	6
10	G	The bottom of the social structure tells us a great deal about the problems Americans faced.

11	Answers will vary, but student's response could include:
	• The numbers of babies and children who died during the epidemics was tragically high.
	• The mortality rate of babies and children as a result of the epidemics was noted to be tragically high.
12	A were commonly found
13	Answers will vary, but student's response could include:
	• It was difficult for anyone to survive the epidemics that were so easily spread throughout the tenements.
14	Answers will vary, but student's response culd include:
	• middle-class city dwellers lived
	• middle-class city dwellers resided
15	Answers will vary, but student's response could include:
	• The middle-class families were contented because they could afford bathing facilities, cookware, and proper lighting to make their homes sanitary and pleasant.
	• The middle-class family could afford bathing facilities, cookware, and proper lighting to make their homes sanitary and pleasant.
16	H composed of
17	D 15
18	F and become breadwinners
19	C 18
20	Answers will vary, but student's response could include:
	• Although women didn't generally enter the workforce, as a group they made themselves heard on matters of civic interest.
21	G after sentence 19
22	Answers will vary, but student's response could include:
	• "Middle-Class Life in America in the 1800s"
23	C
24	G
25	A
26	H
27	D
28	G
29	C
30	J
31	B

Practice Test 4: Social Science

Sample	D	Asia
1	A	the Puritan leader, John Winthrop
2	H	it halted the tax on printed matter circulating in the colonies
3	A	it proclaimed the people's right to abolish unfair governments
4	H	the elevation of American women as moral and civic guides
5		Answers will vary, but student's response could include:
		• they proposed a two-house legislature to balance the interests of large and small states
		• the Three-Fifths Compromise was established whereby only three fifths of a state's slave population would count in determining its representation
6	D	to guarantee specific rights to U.S. citizens
7		Answers will vary, but student's response could include:
		• the plantation is surrounded by natural "fences" such as rivers and marsh land, which would make it difficult for slaves to escape
		• majority of the property was cultivated fields
8	G	the opening of the continent's interior to settlement
9		Answers will vary, but student's response could include:
		• to mobilize into action in order to defend themselves and the land that Tecumseh believed was theirs
10	A	The North was heavily industrialized.
11	H	utopian communities
12	A	to oppose the expansion of slavery into the western territories
13	G	It denied that the federal government had authority to limit slavery.
14	D	It had a good defensive strategy and superior military leadership.
15	H	local officials obtained jobs and services for voters
16		Answers will vary, but student's response could include:
		• changes in unfair business practices
		• improvement in the plight of workers
17	A	Roosevelt wanted to reform government and regulate big business.
18	J	the quest for colonial empires

19	B	the Balkans
20	H	suspected radicals
21	B	the availability of electrical power
22	F	Michigan, Indiana, and Ohio
23	C	large-scale programs which directly helped needy people
24	J	partial isolationism in dealing with foreign countries
25	A	increased production of military vehicles and weaponry
26	G	to stabilize and rebuild Europe after World War II
27	D	returning war veterans
28	G	The Constitution limited a president's tenure to two terms.
29	A	nonviolent protest
30	H	bar discrimination on the basis of sex
31	A	oppose the threat of communism in Southeast Asia
32	G	The White House authorized an illegal break-in to spy on the activities of the Democratic National Committee.
33	A	a secret sale of missiles to Iran authorized by the U.S. administration
34	H	unemployment, the rate of inflation, and interest rates remained low
35	D	Russian expansion was blocked by other empires, but U.S. expansion was not.
36	F	cycles of boom and bust
37		Answers will vary, but student's response could include: • technology has made the world "smaller" in that everyone has fast and easy access to American pop culture
38	C	to investigate and publicize human rights abuses

Practice Test 5: Listening

Sample A	B	the draft
1	B	occurring at the very beginning
2	J	engage for military service
3	C	the state of belonging to neither side
4	F	attend to the needs of others
5	B	on the side of the British
6	H	a system of government run by elected officials
7	B	sail completely around the world
8	G	promises
9	D	banished
10	J	compel
11	B	belief
12	H	inappropriate
13	B	an outbreak of infectious disease
14	F	partnership
15	A	a governor
16	J	relieved

Passage: Southern Opposition to the Civil War

Sample B	C	the conflict lasted longer than anyone had foreseen
17	C	papers giving a person immunity from military duty
18	F	plantation owners avoided military service
19	D	poor farmers and working people
20	H	irresponsible and lazy
21	A	they believed it violated states' rights
22	H	obtaining food from civilians at low cost
23	D	unfair and unconstitutional
24	G	their troops had little food and supplies
25	A	people would have stormed food stores for free food
26	G	"Critics of the Confederacy"

130

Answer Sheet

STUDENT'S NAME — LAST / FIRST / MI

SCHOOL:
TEACHER:
FEMALE ○   MALE ○

BIRTH DATE

MONTH	DAY	YEAR
Jan ○	⓪ ⓪	⓪ ⓪
Feb ○	① ①	① ①
Mar ○	② ②	② ②
Apr ○	③ ③	③ ③
May ○	④	④ ④
Jun ○	⑤	⑤ ⑤
Jul ○	⑥	⑥ ⑥
Aug ○	⑦	⑦ ⑦
Sep ○	⑧	⑧ ⑧
Oct ○	⑨	⑨ ⑨
Nov ○		
Dec ○		

GRADE

Fill in the circle for each multiple-choice answer. Write the answers to the open-ended questions in the space provided.

TEST 1   Reading Comprehension

SA Ⓐ Ⓑ Ⓒ Ⓓ
1. Ⓐ Ⓑ Ⓒ Ⓓ
2. Ⓕ Ⓖ Ⓗ Ⓙ
3. Ⓐ Ⓑ Ⓒ Ⓓ
4. Ⓕ Ⓖ Ⓗ Ⓙ
5. Ⓐ Ⓑ Ⓒ Ⓓ
6. Ⓕ Ⓖ Ⓗ Ⓙ
7. Ⓐ Ⓑ Ⓒ Ⓓ
8. Open-ended
9. Ⓕ Ⓖ Ⓗ Ⓙ
10. Open-ended
11. Ⓐ Ⓑ Ⓒ Ⓓ
12. Ⓕ Ⓖ Ⓗ Ⓙ
13. Ⓐ Ⓑ Ⓒ Ⓓ
14. Ⓕ Ⓖ Ⓗ Ⓙ
15. Ⓐ Ⓑ Ⓒ Ⓓ
16. Ⓕ Ⓖ Ⓗ Ⓙ
17. Ⓐ Ⓑ Ⓒ Ⓓ
18. Open-ended
19. Ⓕ Ⓖ Ⓗ Ⓙ
20. Ⓐ Ⓑ Ⓒ Ⓓ
21. Ⓕ Ⓖ Ⓗ Ⓙ
22. Open-ended
23. Ⓐ Ⓑ Ⓒ Ⓓ
24. Ⓕ Ⓖ Ⓗ Ⓙ
25. Ⓐ Ⓑ Ⓒ Ⓓ
26. Ⓕ Ⓖ Ⓗ Ⓙ
27. Ⓐ Ⓑ Ⓒ Ⓓ
28. Ⓕ Ⓖ Ⓗ Ⓙ
29. Ⓐ Ⓑ Ⓒ Ⓓ
30. Ⓕ Ⓖ Ⓗ Ⓙ
31. Ⓐ Ⓑ Ⓒ Ⓓ
32. Ⓕ Ⓖ Ⓗ Ⓙ
33. Ⓐ Ⓑ Ⓒ Ⓓ
34. Ⓕ Ⓖ Ⓗ Ⓙ
35. Ⓐ Ⓑ Ⓒ Ⓓ
36. Ⓕ Ⓖ Ⓗ Ⓙ
37. Ⓐ Ⓑ Ⓒ Ⓓ

TEST 2   Reading Vocabulary

SA Ⓐ Ⓑ Ⓒ Ⓓ
1. Ⓐ Ⓑ Ⓒ Ⓓ
2. Ⓕ Ⓖ Ⓗ Ⓙ
3. Ⓐ Ⓑ Ⓒ Ⓓ
4. Ⓕ Ⓖ Ⓗ Ⓙ
5. Ⓐ Ⓑ Ⓒ Ⓓ
6. Ⓕ Ⓖ Ⓗ Ⓙ
7. Ⓐ Ⓑ Ⓒ Ⓓ
8. Ⓕ Ⓖ Ⓗ Ⓙ
9. Ⓐ Ⓑ Ⓒ Ⓓ
10. Open-ended

Copyright © by Steck-Vaughn Company. All rights reserved.

TEST 3 Language

SA Ⓐ Ⓑ Ⓒ Ⓓ	6 Open-ended	12 Ⓐ Ⓑ Ⓒ Ⓓ	18 Ⓕ Ⓖ Ⓗ Ⓙ	24 Ⓕ Ⓖ Ⓗ Ⓙ	30 Ⓕ Ⓖ Ⓗ Ⓙ
1 Open-ended	7 Ⓐ Ⓑ Ⓒ Ⓓ	13 Open-ended	19 Ⓐ Ⓑ Ⓒ Ⓓ	25 Ⓐ Ⓑ Ⓒ Ⓓ	31 Ⓐ Ⓑ Ⓒ Ⓓ
2 Ⓐ Ⓑ Ⓒ Ⓓ	8 Ⓕ Ⓖ Ⓗ Ⓙ	14 Open-ended	20 Open-ended	26 Ⓕ Ⓖ Ⓗ Ⓙ	
3 Ⓕ Ⓖ Ⓗ Ⓙ	9 Ⓐ Ⓑ Ⓒ Ⓓ	15 Open-ended	21 Ⓕ Ⓖ Ⓗ Ⓙ	27 Ⓐ Ⓑ Ⓒ Ⓓ	
4 Ⓐ Ⓑ Ⓒ Ⓓ	10 Ⓕ Ⓖ Ⓗ Ⓙ	16 Ⓕ Ⓖ Ⓗ Ⓙ	22 Open-ended	28 Ⓕ Ⓖ Ⓗ Ⓙ	
5 Ⓕ Ⓖ Ⓗ Ⓙ	11 Open-ended	17 Ⓐ Ⓑ Ⓒ Ⓓ	23 Ⓐ Ⓑ Ⓒ Ⓓ	29 Ⓐ Ⓑ Ⓒ Ⓓ	

TEST 4 Social Science

SA Ⓐ Ⓑ Ⓒ Ⓓ	7 Open-ended	14 Ⓐ Ⓑ Ⓒ Ⓓ	21 Ⓐ Ⓑ Ⓒ Ⓓ	28 Ⓕ Ⓖ Ⓗ Ⓙ	35 Ⓐ Ⓑ Ⓒ Ⓓ
1 Ⓐ Ⓑ Ⓒ Ⓓ	8 Ⓕ Ⓖ Ⓗ Ⓙ	15 Ⓕ Ⓖ Ⓗ Ⓙ	22 Ⓕ Ⓖ Ⓗ Ⓙ	29 Ⓐ Ⓑ Ⓒ Ⓓ	36 Ⓕ Ⓖ Ⓗ Ⓙ
2 Ⓕ Ⓖ Ⓗ Ⓙ	9 Open-ended	16 Open-ended	23 Ⓐ Ⓑ Ⓒ Ⓓ	30 Ⓕ Ⓖ Ⓗ Ⓙ	37 Open-ended
3 Ⓐ Ⓑ Ⓒ Ⓓ	10 Ⓐ Ⓑ Ⓒ Ⓓ	17 Ⓐ Ⓑ Ⓒ Ⓓ	24 Ⓕ Ⓖ Ⓗ Ⓙ	31 Ⓐ Ⓑ Ⓒ Ⓓ	38 Ⓐ Ⓑ Ⓒ Ⓓ
4 Ⓕ Ⓖ Ⓗ Ⓙ	11 Ⓕ Ⓖ Ⓗ Ⓙ	18 Ⓕ Ⓖ Ⓗ Ⓙ	25 Ⓐ Ⓑ Ⓒ Ⓓ	32 Ⓕ Ⓖ Ⓗ Ⓙ	
5 Open-ended	12 Ⓐ Ⓑ Ⓒ Ⓓ	19 Ⓐ Ⓑ Ⓒ Ⓓ	26 Ⓕ Ⓖ Ⓗ Ⓙ	33 Ⓐ Ⓑ Ⓒ Ⓓ	
6 Ⓐ Ⓑ Ⓒ Ⓓ	13 Ⓕ Ⓖ Ⓗ Ⓙ	20 Ⓕ Ⓖ Ⓗ Ⓙ	27 Ⓐ Ⓑ Ⓒ Ⓓ	34 Ⓕ Ⓖ Ⓗ Ⓙ	

TEST 5 Listening

SA Ⓐ Ⓑ Ⓒ Ⓓ	6 Ⓕ Ⓖ Ⓗ Ⓙ	12 Ⓕ Ⓖ Ⓗ Ⓙ	SB Ⓐ Ⓑ Ⓒ Ⓓ	22 Ⓕ Ⓖ Ⓗ Ⓙ
1 Ⓐ Ⓑ Ⓒ Ⓓ	7 Ⓐ Ⓑ Ⓒ Ⓓ	13 Ⓐ Ⓑ Ⓒ Ⓓ	17 Ⓐ Ⓑ Ⓒ Ⓓ	23 Ⓐ Ⓑ Ⓒ Ⓓ
2 Ⓕ Ⓖ Ⓗ Ⓙ	8 Ⓕ Ⓖ Ⓗ Ⓙ	14 Ⓕ Ⓖ Ⓗ Ⓙ	18 Ⓕ Ⓖ Ⓗ Ⓙ	24 Ⓕ Ⓖ Ⓗ Ⓙ
3 Ⓐ Ⓑ Ⓒ Ⓓ	9 Ⓐ Ⓑ Ⓒ Ⓓ	15 Ⓐ Ⓑ Ⓒ Ⓓ	19 Ⓐ Ⓑ Ⓒ Ⓓ	25 Ⓐ Ⓑ Ⓒ Ⓓ
4 Ⓕ Ⓖ Ⓗ Ⓙ	10 Ⓕ Ⓖ Ⓗ Ⓙ	16 Ⓕ Ⓖ Ⓗ Ⓙ	20 Ⓕ Ⓖ Ⓗ Ⓙ	26 Ⓕ Ⓖ Ⓗ Ⓙ
5 Ⓐ Ⓑ Ⓒ Ⓓ	11 Ⓐ Ⓑ Ⓒ Ⓓ		21 Ⓐ Ⓑ Ⓒ Ⓓ	

Copyright © by Steck-Vaughn Company. All rights reserved.